DEVELOPMENTAL PSYCHOBIOLOGY
the significance of infancy

Contributors

Joseph J. Campos
Daniel G. Freedman
Jerome Kagan
Lewis P. Lipsitt
Sandra Scarr-Salapatek
Philip Zelazo

DEVELOPMENTAL PSYCHOBIOLOGY

the significance of infancy

EDITED BY

LEWIS P. LIPSITT

BROWN UNIVERSITY

LAWRENCE ERLBAUM ASSOCIATES, PUBLISHERS
1976 Hillsdale, New Jersey

DISTRIBUTED BY THE HALSTED PRESS DIVISION OF

JOHN WILEY & SONS

New York Toronto London Sydney

Lawrence Erlbaum Associates, Inc., Publishers
62 Maria Drive
Hillsdale, New Jersey 07642

Distributed solely by Halsted Press Division
John Wiley & Sons, Inc., New York

Library of Congress Cataloging in Publication Data

Main entry under title:

Developmental psychobiology.

Includes bibliographical references and index.
1. Infant psychology. 2. Developmental psychobiology. I. Lipsitt, Lewis Paeff, 1929–
BF723.16D39 155.4'22 76-14775
ISBN 0-470-15127-7

April 19, 1976

Printed in the United States of America

Contents

Preface

This volume is based on a symposium of the same title held in San Francisco at the 1974 meetings of the American Association for the Advancement of Science (AAAS). The half-day session was sponsored jointly by the Society for Research in Child Development and the Section on Psychology of the AAAS. I served as chairman of the session and then as discussant.

The field of developmental psychobiology acknowledges that a union of the sciences of biology and psychology is essential for a better understanding of the wondrous ways in which experience interacts with congenital factors to produce growth, development, or change. The contributors to this volume are all committed to such an interactionist orientation with respect to both the origins of infant behavior and the role of infancy in the determination of later development.

The symposium participants did not make their oral presentations, or engage in discussion with their fellow panel members, with a view toward publication of the proceedings. However, it became apparent at the time of the symposium that there was a great deal of interest in the topic of developmental psychobiology and that there was not enough time to engage in as much cross-communication among the panelists as we all wanted. Members of the audience also voiced their frustration, on termination of the three-hour session, that the panelists had too little opportunity to question and to respond to one another. Although it has not been possible to incorporate audience participation and panel responses, except to take that interchange into consideration in the preparation of our contributions to this volume, the major presentations were followed by lively queries from the audience.

Whereas the participants were aware, going into the meeting, that there were important differences among them, they did not anticipate that they would probably have enough to say to one another to warrant a session at least twice the length of the one planned. There were important differences as to which developmental data we wanted to attend to most. Among other matters, these differences concerned our respective scientific orientations and "world views" on the "nature–nurture" issue. In different ways, each of our contributions has something to say about the problem, and about the specific ways in which experience imposes itself on the genetic substrate.

The symposium speakers have expanded their presentations. It was decided also that each panelist would provide a commentary on one of the other presentations, in hopes that this would result in a lively interaction that could now go beyond even the excitement generated on the occasion of the original oral presentations. I have contributed a discussion that seeks to reflect on the other contributions to the volume. I hoped also to call attention to the burgeoning field of the psychobiology of infancy by citing some findings from my own laboratory that bear on principles and empirical issues raised by the other contributions.

Finally, the symposium participants have been joined by Jerome Kagan, who has written an Epilogue for the volume.

LEWIS P. LIPSITT

1

Heart Rate: A Sensitive Tool for the Study of Emotional Development in the Infant

Joseph J. Campos

University of Denver

Psychophysiological responses seem to be especially well suited to the study of the human infant. First, they are extremely sensitive to changes in psychological state, often more so than behavioral measures. The electroencephalogram (EEG), for example, can differentiate states of sleep that are not readily discriminable from behavioral observations alone (Rechtschaffen & Kales, 1968). Second, physiological responses are nonverbal and so are of particular benefit in studies of nonverbal subjects, such as infants. Third, they have an impressive history in studies of learning, habituation, psychophysics, and emotion. As a result, the parameters affecting these responses are often better known than the parameters affecting less studied responses. Fourth, they can be used in longitudinal studies in ways in which overt, coordinated behavioral responses cannot, either because the physiological response is already functional at birth or because the emergence of the response reflects important biological milestones [for example, the development of the EEG K complex (Emde, Gaensbauer, & Harmon, 1976)].

WHY HEART RATE RESPONSES ARE WIDELY USED WITH INFANTS

Many physiological responses have been used in infant studies; of all of these, heart rate (HR) has proved the most sensitive and reliable. In this chapter, some of the major research areas in which HR has been fruitfully studied in infants are briefly reviewed. Then a series of studies is described, suggesting that the HR response can be very useful in detecting developmental shifts in emotional and perceptual reactions in infancy.

Some of the other physiological responses that have been used successfully with adults have proved to be less helpful in studies of the infant. Most disappointing in this regard are probably the electrodermal measures—skin conductance and skin potential. Crowell, Davis, Chun, and Spellacy (1965) reported obtaining skin conductance responses in newborns, on the average, to only 18% of the stimuli they used, despite the fact that their stimuli effectively elicited behavioral responses. This is a much lower percentage than that expected from studies of adults. Campos, Tursky, and Conway (1971) also reported finding little evidence of skin conductance reactivity in young infants. Although Stechler, Bradford, and Levy (1966) reported finding skin potential responses to a puff of nitrogen applied to the abdomen of neonates, Appel (1971) and Conway (1972) simultaneously recorded both skin potential and HR responses to a wide variety of stimuli and found HR to be much more reactive response in young infants.

Many of the other physiological responses favored in studies of adults, such as pupillography (Fitzgerald, 1968), psychoendocrinology (Tennes & Carter, 1973), and plethysmography (the measurement of blood flow), are intrusive measures that require restraint of the infant's arms, feet, or head or painful pricking of the skin.

The electroencephalograph has been successfully used in studies of infants (e.g., Anders, Emde, & Parmelee, 1971; Ellingson, 1960; Emde *et al.,* in press), but the interest in this response deals with the identification of the ages at which different features develop. The neonatal EEG, for example, has not been found to discriminate reliably between waking and active sleep (Anders *et al.*, 1971), nor between various nonsleep REM states (Emde & Metcalf, 1970).

Heart rate, however, has a number of advantages in research with infants. First of all, there is a reasonably well-developed clinical literature relating fetal cardiac responses to stress, especially the stress of labor and delivery (Hon, 1959). Lipton, Steinschneider, and Richmond (1965) have reported it to be very reactive to such conditions as uterine contractions, maternal exercise, and anoxia. Apgar (1953) considers HR to be one of the significant clinical features to concentrate on in ratings of the infant's condition at birth.

Second, HR responses, which can be recorded relatively unobtrusively in infants with only three small leads attached carefully to the chest, have been found in numerous studies to be very sensitive to a number of important psychological variables. Of these, the most important are state, auditory sensitivity, individual differences, and conditioning.

State. State is the condition of the organism ranging from deep sleep, through the awake and alert state, to fussiness and crying. Both Bridger, Birns, and Blank (1965) and Campos and Brackbill (1973) have found HR levels to be highly related to behavioral ratings of state: As the overall excitation level of the infant increases, so does HR level, with remarkable ordinal precision. However, both studies also reported that the relationship between HR and state is not such that one can infer state from HR level alone, because two infants with the same HR level were not necessarily in the same state.

Both soothing stimuli and incentives seem to affect HR levels. Birns, Blank, and Bridger (1966) and Brackbill (1971) have shown how soothing stimuli affect HR levels. In Brackbill's study, the effect was particularly pronounced. She reported finding a significant linear decrease in HR with increasing number of modalities that received continuous stimulation. However, working with incentives, Lipsitt (this volume) has reported recently that HR levels during sucking for sucrose solution increase significantly above those of nonnutritive sucking. Therefore the infant's HR may increase or decrease as a function of incentive–motivational conditions.

Auditory sensitivity. Heart rate has been found to be useful in the study of auditory sensitivity in the neonate. Both Bartoshuk (1964) and Steinschneider, Lipton, and Richmond (1966) reported increases in the magnitude of HR response with increase in stimulus intensity. Bridger (1961) has used HR in a habituation–dishabituation paradigm and has reported successful discrimination by the neonate of 400-Hz and 1,000-Hz tones. Stratton and Connolly (1973) also reported evidence for pitch discrimination through measurement of cardiac response dishabituation in neonates.

Individual differences. Although the test–retest reliability of various HR response parameters has not always been found to be sufficiently high for use as tests of individual differences (Clifton & Graham, 1968), several studies have shown stable individual differences of sufficient magnitude to warrant further research. Bridger and Reiser (1959) reported 24-hr retest reliabilities of several of these parameters of HR and found reliability coefficients as high as .96 (for average HR level reached during stimulation). Despite fairly small sample sizes, Lipton, Steinschneider, and Richmond (1966) have reported a number of significantly stable individual differences on HR response measures between the ages of 2½ and 5 months. Clifton and Graham (1968), despite their disclaimer about the use of HR as a discriminator of individuals, nevertheless also reported stability in some HR measures in newborns retested for up to 5 days.

Conditioning. Recent evidence suggests that HR can be used successfully in studies of classical conditioning in infants. Porges and his students (Porges, 1974) have recently reported that anticipatory cardiac deceleration can be elicited in female neonates by using a trace conditioning paradigm with an auditory conditioned stimulus and a visual unconditioned stimulus. Furthermore, they reported finding deceleration in both sexes of newborn infants when the unconditioned stimulus failed to follow the conditioned stimulus. However, one study of operant conditioning of HR in infants 12, 24, and 36 months of age, obtained negative results (Silverman & Campos, 1973).

BIDIRECTIONAL NATURE OF THE HEART RATE RESPONSE

Perhaps the most significant reason for the importance of HR in the study of the infant is the feature of bidirectional cardiac responding. That is, HR can increase or decrease in response to stimulation, and several theoretical considerations have led psychophysiologists to attribute different psychological functions to the two directions of change possible with HR.

Prior to the innovative work by the Laceys (e.g., Lacey & Lacey, 1958), most psychophysiologists interpreted brief (phasic) cardiac accelerations or longer lasting (tonic) increases in HR level as indications of the organism's level of activation (Duffy, 1962; Malmo, 1959), or preparation for fight or flight (Cannon, 1927). Such activation had been theorized to facilitate sensory and motoric activity through the mediation of the reticular formation (Lindsley, 1951). In 1958, however, Lacey and Lacey reviewed evidence indicating that for cardiovascular responses, such as HR and blood pressure, increases in activity led to inhibitory rather than facilitatory effects on cortical arousal, contrary to the predictions of activation theorists. The Laceys described a negative-feedback system involving baroreceptor afferent stimulation from the aortic arch and carotid sinus (among other places) to the nucleus tractus solitarius, a region that has been shown to exert inhibitory control over cortical activity (Bonvallet & Bloch, 1961; Bonvallet & Allen, 1963). Because every single heartbeat causes an increase in firing of the baroreceptors (and, by extrapolation, of the nucleus tractus solitarius), Lacey and Lacey have predicted that decreases in the frequency of firing of the baroreceptors (such as by decrease in HR) should lead to decreased cortical inhibition and thus to improved sensory and motoric activity. Increases, in contrast, should lead to poorer sensory and motoric activity. In a number of studies (e.g., Lacey & Lacey, 1970), these predictions have been confirmed: a small but consistent relationship has been found between decreases in HR and faster reaction time.

The Laceys have also related the direction of HR response to the organism's intended transaction with the environment (Lacey, Kagan, Lacey, & Moss, 1963). Those situations involving sensory intake, or close attention to the environment, according to the Laceys, produce HR slowing. Those involving rejection of the environment, blocking out of painful, distressing, or distracting stimulation, produce HR accelerations. Although a number of objections have been raised to the Laceys' theory (Elliot, 1972; Hahn, 1973), several studies of adult subjects have confirmed that in at least some conditions of attention to the environment, HR slows down, whereas it frequently accelerates to problem-solving tasks and certain stressors, such as the cold pressor test (Obrist, 1963).

Graham and Clifton (1966) linked the Lacey's neurophysiological reasoning to Sokolov's (1963) theory of orienting and defensive reflexes. Sokolov had postulated that the orienting reflex (which could be elicited by brief, low- to moderate-intensity simple sensory stimuli) served to enhance sensory receptivity, whereas the defensive reflex limited the effects of painful or intense stimulation.

Graham and Clifton, noting that Sokolov had tended to ignore HR responses, postulated that HR deceleration might be an index of the orienting reflex or response and thereby assist, by means of the Laceys' proposed neurophysiological mechanism, the enhancement of sensory input. Heart rate acceleration, in contrast, was linked to the defensive response, startle, and other conditions of noxious stimulation.

Still another interpretation of the bidirectional nature of the cardiac response is that of Obrist (Obrist, Webb, Sutterer, & Howard, 1970). It is very different from that of both the Laceys and Graham and Clifton. Although recognizing that HR typically slows down in conditions of attentiveness, Obrist explains the direction of HR change not in connection with hypothetical cardiovascular feedback mechanisms, nor with orienting versus defensive arousal systems, but in terms of the metabolic demands of the body musculature. For example, when a person is very attentive to the environment HR slows down because, under those conditions, motoric activity is typically inhibited. When a person behaves defensively, however, he usually cringes, turns away, shows evidence of motoric excitement, and HR accelerates in synchrony with the increase in motoric activity.

Whether linked conceptually to "attention to the environment," to the orienting response, or to the demands of the body musculature, all of which generally covary in the intact subject, HR deceleratory responses soon began to attract the attention of numerous researchers. For some, the interest grew out of the paradoxical nature of the HR decelerations obtained by the Laceys under conditions of activation. For others, the role of attention and orienting in learning in children (House & Zeaman, 1963; Lynn, 1966) soon brought the study of the response to the age level of infancy.

By now, the linkage between cardiac deceleratory responses and attention or orienting in the infant is well accepted, as a result of the studies (among many others) by Kagan and Lewis (1965), Lewis, Kagan, Campbell, and Kalafat (1966), and Graham (e.g., Graham, Berg, Berg, Jackson, Hatton, & Kantowitz, 1970). The HR deceleratory response, for example, has been found to occur in infants paying close attention to auditory and visual displays (Lewis *et al.,* 1966; Lewis & Spaulding, 1967). It occurs to stimuli discrepant from an infant's past experience (Kagan, 1968; Lewis & Goldberg, 1969). It has been found to habituate, a criterion of the orienting response according to Sokolov, in studies by Merryweather, Campos, Schwartz, and Flanders (1973), and Horowitz (1972) among others. Decelerations also occur to either the onset or the offset of stimulation, another criterion of orienting (Lewis, 1971). Furthermore, it is now becoming clear that even neonates, under certain circumstances, can give deceleratory orienting response if they are presented with a visual target on which to fixate (Sameroff, Cashmore, & Dykes, 1973) or, in infants categorized as having high resting HR variability, with the offset of a long-duration auditory stimulus (Porges, Arnold, & Forbes, 1973). Lipsitt and Jacklin (1971) and Kearsley (1973) have also obtained evidence for cardiac deceleratory orienting responses in newborns.

With one exception, the investigation in infants of the cardiac acceleratory response postulated to be a component of the defensive reaction or of rejection of the environment has proceeded much more slowly than investigation of HR decelerations. The exception is the cardiac acceleration obtained with brief sensory stimuli, which Graham and her co-workers (e.g., Graham & Jackson, 1970) have repeatedly observed in neonates even to stimuli that elicit large-magnitude decelerations in older infants (Graham *et al.,* 1970).

RECENT STUDIES OF HEART RATE RESPONSIVENESS IN PERCEPTUAL SETTINGS

Recent trends indicate an increased interest in cardiac acceleratory responses in human infants. A research project in which the bidirectionality of the infant's HR response has proved particularly useful in our laboratory concerns the testing of an infant's fear of depth atop the visual cliff. Ever since the time of Berkeley and Hume in the early eighteenth century, philosophers and psychologists have speculated about the perceptual experience of the human infant. The perception of depth, for many psychologists, was an experience that depended on learning to associate visual input with touch. The very young infant, therefore, in whom touch and vision are not evidently intercorrelated (Piaget, 1951), should not be able to perceive depth. In the mid-1960s, Bower (1964, 1965, 1966) had excited the imagination of psychologists by demonstrating, with an operant conditioning technique, that the 2-month-old infant possesses size and shape constancy and so can perceive depth at an age far younger than anyone had succeeded previously in demonstrating or than empiricist theories would have led us to believe. Unfortunately, in the time that has elapsed since Bower's research appeared, problems with the research have come to light. For example, the operant conditioning task required the infant to make one head turn every 2 sec for 15 min, which creates a very heavy demand on a 2-month-old infant and which makes the design very impractical with even younger infants. Second, a number of investigators reportedly have had difficulty in replicating the learning procedure used in these studies.

The visual cliff, developed in the late 1950s at Cornell University by Walk and Gibson (1961), provided a simple alternative to Bower's method for studying infant depth perception. The apparatus consists of a large, Herculite–glass covered table, with two halves, one called the "deep" side, with a checkered surface placed on the floor, some 40 inches below the glass tabletop. The other is the "shallow" side, with the checkered surface placed immediately below the glass. Testing for depth perception was done by Gibson and Walk by placing a subject on a board straddling the two sides of the cliff and observing which side the subject chooses to cross over to get to his mother. The apparatus has been extremely useful in studies of many different species, and has elicited fear of depth in animals as young as 1 day. So long as the visual cliff method relied on locomotor responses for the testing of human infants, it could not say much about the aversiveness of depth in humans before the age of locomotion. However, there is a simple method that does not require locomotion for testing subjects on the visual cliff. By measuring differences in emotional reactions of subjects placed directly atop the deep or the shallow side, it is possible to test very young subjects. Gibson and Walk (1960) have reported testing kittens, chickens, and infant goats in this way with the result that subjects placed directly atop the deep side of the cliff showed evidence of distress.

Because the visual cliff is so much simpler a situation than Bower's, and because cardiac acceleration indicative of distress, startle, or defensiveness can be elicited even in newborns, it has seemed worthwhile to determine whether distress or defensive responses can be elicited on the visual cliff at the same ages for which Bower has reported the presence of size and shape constancy. Furthermore, the visual cliff provides a simple enough situation to be useful even with infants much younger than those Bower has tested, providing a method that can tell us the "threshold age" when the infant can first be shown to react to depth.

We conducted a number of such visual cliff studies, using HR and direct placement atop the cliff, in our laboratory at the University of Denver and have come to the conclusion, as a result of the bidirectional nature of the cardiac response, that regardless of the prelocomotor infant's ability to perceive depth, he does not seem to be afraid of it until approximately the age at which he can locomote.

When we tested prelocomotor infants with the direct-placement procedure, we expected the subject to show no significant cardiac response on the shallow side of the cliff. Except possibly for the feel of the glass surface, the shallow side was not too different from many other surfaces in which an infant has been likely to be placed. On the deep side, we expected to observe cardiac accelerations and other signs of aversive and defensive behavior, such as crying and turning of the head away from the deep side.

We were surprised to find that when placed on the deep side of the cliff, groups of 55-day-old and 106-day-old infants showed cardiac decelerations (as well as evidence of suppression of crying) (Campos, Langer, & Krowitz, 1970). The HR data obtained by systematic time sampling during the prestimulus and stimulus presentation periods with the 55-day-old infants are presented in Figure 1.1. Averaged across all the time-sampling points, the HR deceleration during the direct placement over the deep side was 6.10 beats per minute (BPM) in the older group, and 4.70 BPM in the younger ($p < .01$ in each case). Despite the apparent acceleration on the shallow side, the HR change did not approach significance at this age. (Nor did it with the 3-month-olds, who gave a nonsignificant mean HR change of only —.80 BPM on the shallow side). The responses on the deep side were also very consistent between individuals. Of 31 subjects tested at these two ages, 27 gave deceleratory trends on the deep side. Furthermore, at both ages, both the deceleration on the deep side and the discrimination between the two sides were highly significant.

The nature of the cardiac response indicated that the 2- and 3-month-old infants were attentive on the deep side. Could it be that their attentiveness was a function of the stimuli used to serve as surface textures on deep side and shallow sides? Concurrent studies being performed in a number of laboratories were pointing to the importance of contour density in stimulus patterns as a determinant of visual fixation in infancy (Karmel, 1969). Because the same size checkerboard elements were used on the deep and shallow side, the deep side projects more contour density

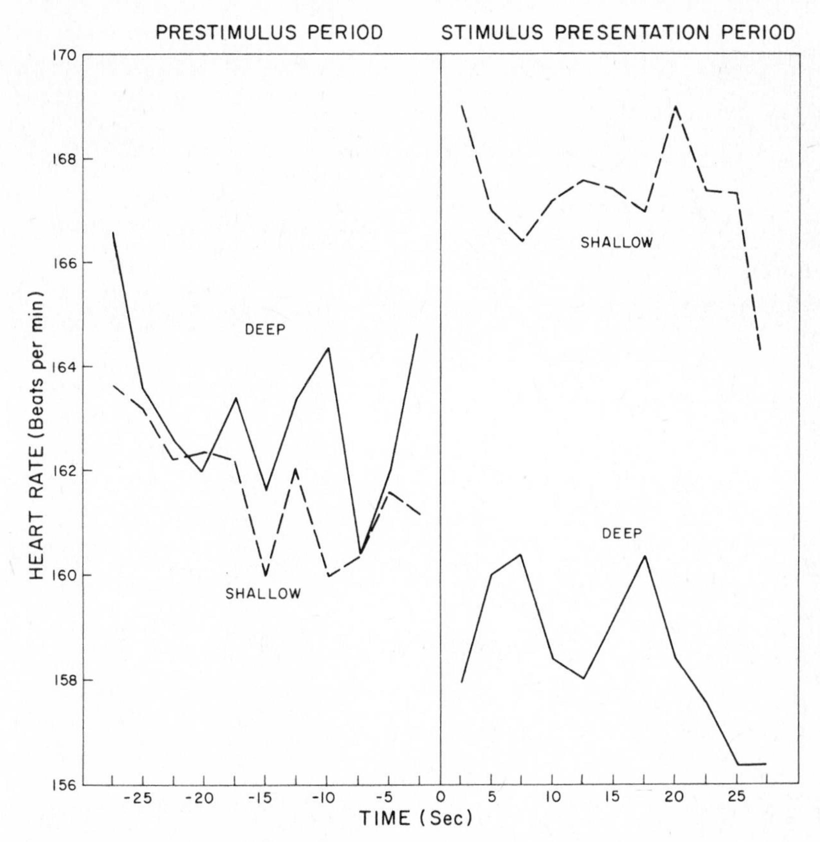

FIGURE 1.1 Cardiac responses of 55-day-old infants on the visual cliff. The apparent acceleration on the shallow side is not statistically significant. (Data from Campos, Langer, & Krowitz, 1970.)

on the retina and so could elicit more attention. To determine whether this was a possibility and to relate these visual cliff studies to those of Bower on discrimination of real size with retinal size held constant, we modified the patterns used on the visual cliff surfaces. By making the checkerboard squares smaller on the shallow side and larger on the deep side, we could equate the retinal densities on the two sides of the cliff from the standpoint of the infant's normal eye position during testing. Even with this control, we found no significant cardiac response on the shallow side (mean HR change = —.39 BPM), significant decelerations on the deep (mean HR change across scoring intervals = —5.36 BPM, $p < .001$), and significant discrimination between the two sides. The mean HR data obtained at each scoring interval during prestimulus and stimulus presentation periods are shown in Figure 1.2. Importantly, we again found the orienting component of the HR response, HR deceleration, no behavioral

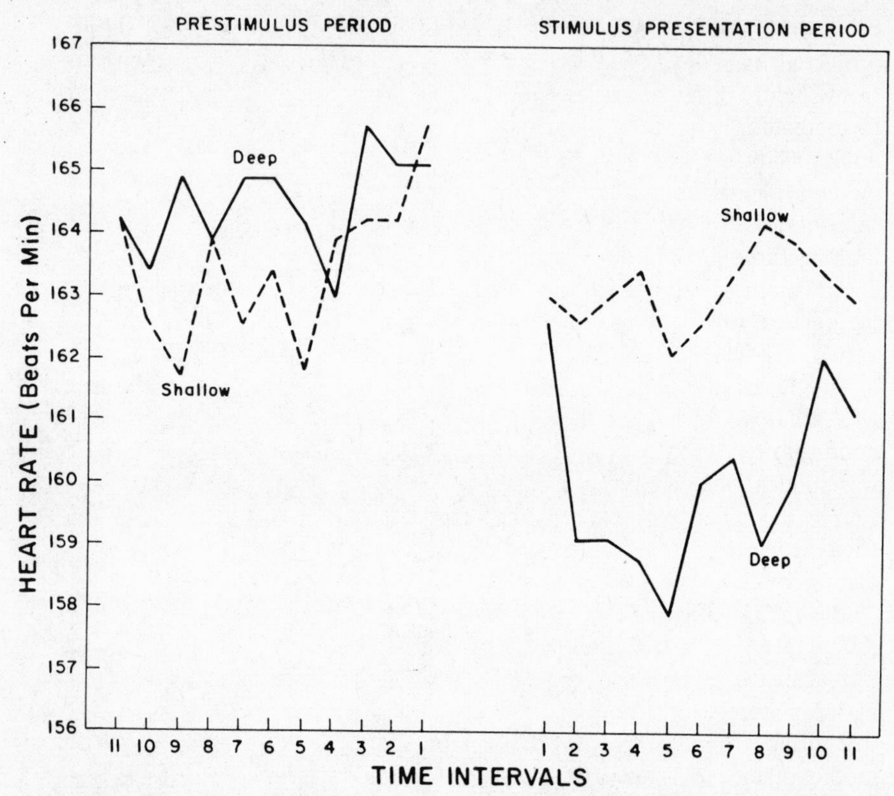

FIGURE 1.2 Cardiac responses of 2-month-old infants on the visual cliff with retinal size held constant. The units on the abscissa refer to 2.5-sec scoring intervals. To minimize effects of handling of the infant, the initial 2.5-sec interval was not scored for either period. (Data from Campos & Langer, 1971.)

evidence of distress, and very consistent responding across individuals (19 of 23 subjects manifesting the same trend as the group data).

In order to determine whether the discrimination we were obtaining in 2-month-old infants was specific to the visual cliff, Appel (1971) studied whether the human infant could detect and differentially respond to binocular disparity with all other depth-specifying information held constant. Appel's study involved the use of the habituation–dishabituation paradigm. To control for all depth-related cues but binocular disparity (the slightly different image each eye receives from fixating the same object from slightly different locations), she used stereoscopic projection equipment and a specially devised set of polaroid glasses for the infant to wear. The projector cast two images on a screen, one through one set of polarizing filters and one through a second set. When wearing the polaroid spectacles, the infant had one of the two images on the screen blocked out of vision in one eye and the other image blocked out in the other eye. By projecting two images on the screen (pictures of a blue toy rabbit taken from slightly different angles with a stereoscopic camera), she could therefore create for the infant the condition of binocular disparity, which in the adult elicits such a powerful illusion of depth. In contrast, when two pictures photographed from the same vantage point are projected on the screen, no disparity is created in the two eyes and the adult observer looking through polaroid spectacles sees a flat image. Note that with this design motion parallax, interposition cues in the picture, and the size of the picture are controlled in the study, and only binocular disparity is varied.

The research design used by Appel sought to answer two questions: (1) What would happen if, after a series of trials in which the infant saw nondisparity (i.e., flat to an adult) presentation of the picture, the display was suddenly changed to a disparity display? (2) The second question was simply the reverse of the first: What would happen if, after a series of trials in which the infant saw a display that included retinal disparity, the display was changed to have no disparity?

Group 2D–3D had six presentations of the slides projected with no retinal disparity (2D), followed by two trials in which the pictures had retinal disparity (3D). Group 3D–2D, in contrast, had six presentations of the picture with disparity, followed by two with no disparity. Two control groups were presented with the same stimulus (3D in one case, 2D in the other) for eight trials. A fifth group was presented a single flat (Kodak Carousel-type) slide for eight trials, with no glasses, simply to estimate the effects of wearing the polaroid eyeglasses.

Recording HR and sucking behavior, Appel found that when the stimulus was changed from a nondisparity display to one containing disparity, HR decelerated significantly more and sucking was more suppressed than in the appropriate control group.[1] No such effect was found when the stimulus was switched from disparity to nondisparity (see Figures 1.3 and 1.4). Reasoning that the switch from 2D to 3D was more of a salient condition than the opposite, Appel concluded that 2-month-old infants could perceive the difference between retinal disparity and retinal nondisparity.

With both the visual cliff and the much more complicated dishabituation paradigm, therefore, the results with 2-month-olds indicate that infants of this age are capable of reacting differentially to stimuli that specify depth to adults. However, this finding does not necessarily imply that infants are perceiving depth. Because the 2-month olds did not show any evidence of fear on the deep side, the logic of inferring depth perception

[1] Appel also measured skin potential responses but her interest in this measure had no relevance to the study of binocular disparity.

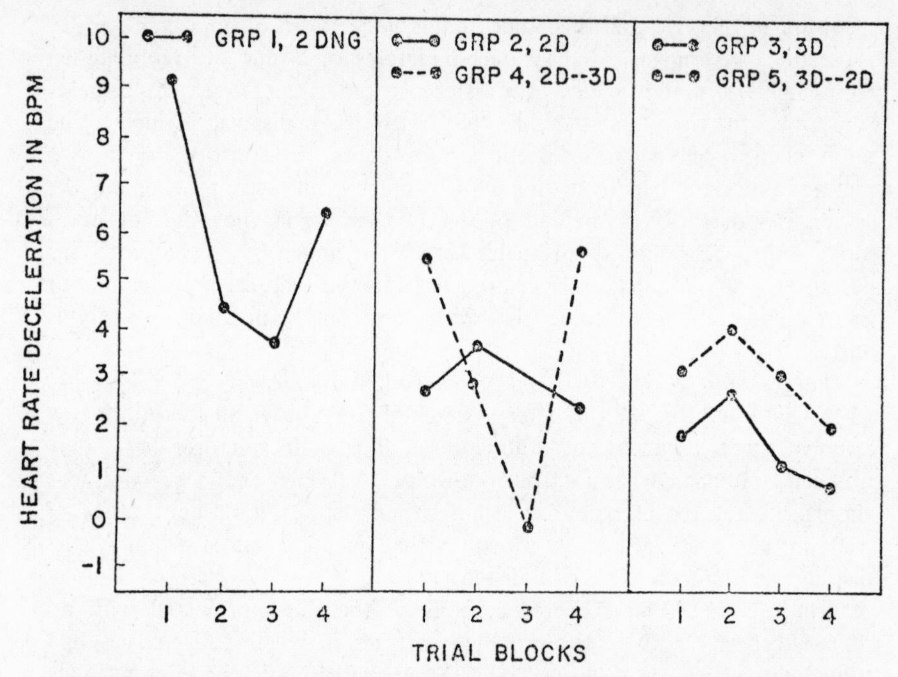

FIGURE 1.3 Cardiac responses of 2-month infants (in trial blocks of two) from Appel's (1971) binocular disparity study. Groups 4 and 5 are the experimental groups. Groups 2 and 3 are the main control groups. Analysis of a significant Group by Trial Blocks interaction revealed a significant change only for Group 4 between Trial Blocks 3 and 4.

from manifestation of fear of heights in infants could not apply at this age. It is possible that infants perceive depth but are not afraid of it; it is also possible that they discriminate a difference in the stimulating circumstances but do not process the difference into experience in the third dimension. Other methods must test which possibility holds true.

To the extent that the previous research obtained evidence for discrimination of depth-specifying stimuli, the question still remained whether younger infants could discriminate the deep and shallow side of the cliff. We therefore studied the cardiac reactions of 4-week-old infants with the same procedure and equipment used with 8-week-olds by Campos *et al.* (1970). Retinal size was not held constant on the two sides. In contrast to the findings obtained with older infants, 4-week-old subjects gave no significant cardiac response on the deep side, nor was there any evidence of discrimination of the deep from the shallow sides at this age.

These results with 4-week olds could not be accounted for by the absence of a capacity for cardiac deceleration in these subjects. Graham and Jackson (1970) had reported difficulty in obtaining decelerations to

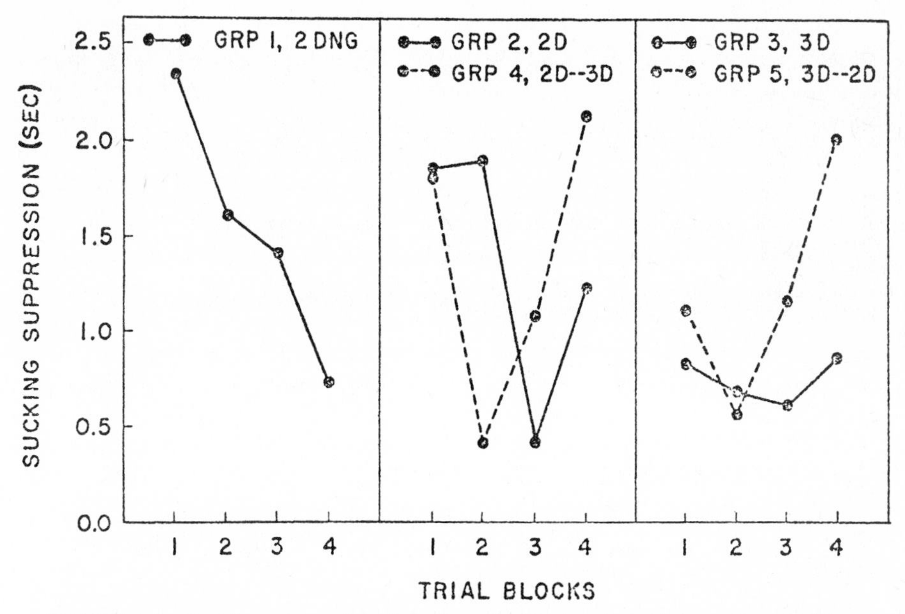

FIGURE 1.4 Sucking suppression data (in trial blocks of two) from Appel's binocular disparity study. Analysis of a significant trial blocks effect demonstrated a significant increase in sucking suppression only for Group 4.

auditory stimuli with subjects in the first 2 months of life. In the present study, however, almost every infant tested displayed periods of deceleration during behavioral recordings of visual attention. However, these periods of close attentiveness were evenly divided between the deep and the shallow sides. It is possible that at this age, as Haynes, White, and Held (1965) suggest, the infants may simply have had difficulty resolving stimuli presented some 40 inches away, as the deep side of the visual cliff is. Other tests of depth perception, therefore, may still prove positive at this age. Nevertheless, the same visual cliff test gives very different results at 4 and 8 weeks of age: no evidence for discrimination at 4 weeks, and very consistent evidence of discrimination at 8 weeks.

Why should infants who so evidently discriminate the two sides of the visual cliff nevertheless not show fear of the deep? Rosenblum and Cross (1963) had reported fearful behaviors in neonatal rhesus monkeys placed on the deep side. Why, then, should 2-month-olds decelerate on the deep side? Was there any possibility, contrary to our interpretation so far, that the 2-month-old is indeed frightened by the deep side but shows this fear with cardiac deceleration?

Because the visual cliff was a very powerful elicitor of avoidance behavior in older infants on trials in which the infant was urged to cross to the mother over the deep side, we decided to test 5- and 9-month-old infants with the direct-placement technique. Certainly, by 9 months of age, one would expect fear of direct placement on the deep side to be manifested, because by this age infants overwhelmingly have shown preference to avoid crawling down onto the deep side (Walk & Gibson, 1961).

As can be seen in Figure 1.5, we (Schwartz, Campos, & Baisel, 1973) discovered that at 5 months of age infants again decelerated on the deep side, although this time much less reliably so and with less magnitude of deceleration as well (mean HR change averaged across intervals = −3.10 BPM, p = NS). However, at 9 months of age, the infant HR shifted to acceleration on the deep side (mean HR change averaged across intervals = +5.3 BPM, $p < .01$) and showed significant differentiation between the two sides as well ($p < .03$) by analysis of covariance performed to remove linear effects of differing prestimulus HR on the response measures. The reaction of infants on the deep side of the visual cliff is therefore very different at different ages and is precisely that expected if what we have stumbled on with these studies is a shift from nonfearfulness on the deep side to fearfulness.

A similar conclusion had previously been drawn by Scarr and Salapatek (1970). In a study of infant reactions to the visual cliff, as well as a number of other stressors, Scarr and Salapatek reported a gradual increase with age in fearfulness of crossing the cliff, as well as no evidence of fear

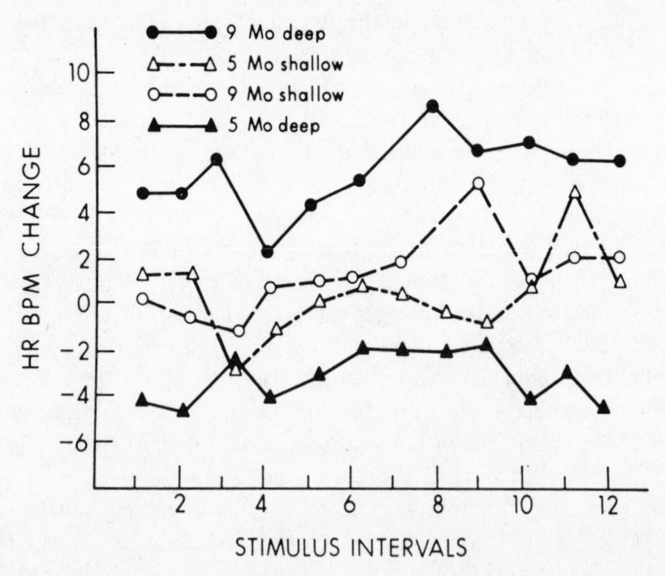

FIGURE 1.5 Cardiac responses (in BPM change) on the visual cliff in 5- and 9-month-old infants. HR was scored every 2.5 sec for 30 sec. (Data from Schwartz, Campos, & Baisel, 1973.)

on direct placement atop the deep side. Despite the congruence of our results with those of Scarr and Salapatek, our conclusions depended entirely on the use of the HR response as the indicator of distress. Our behavioral measures of distress in these studies generally gave us nonsignificant results, which underscored the relatively greater sensitivity of the cardiac response but made it difficult to interpret the HR responses persuasively. Many psychophysiologists would be wary of equating HR acceleration with distress because of a widely obtained phenomenon occurring in classical aversive conditioning studies. When a neutral CS is paired with a shock UCS, the shock elicits a large acceleration of HR, but the anticipatory conditioned response, which numerous learning theorists (e.g., Mowrer, 1960) have postulated as the basis of "fear," is a cardiac deceleration (Bersh, Notterman, & Schoenfeld, 1956; Obrist, Wood, & Perez-Reyez, 1965). These studies then lead to caution in interpreting HR by itself as indicating fear or distress. Schwartz *et al.* (1973) had reported correlations of HR with several behavioral indicators of distress on the visual cliff and had concluded that the pattern of correlations did indeed indicate that HR acceleration was going along with distress. For example, HR change correlated +.38 with distress vocalization and —.30 with ratings of visual attention. However, in the absence of better behavioral data with which to anchor the HR response, the interpretation of our studies of the developmenal shift on the visual cliff remained vulnerable.

VALIDATION OF THE HEART RATE RESPONSE SHIFT: HEART RATE AND STRANGER DISTRESS

Fortunately, there is another developmental shift in infancy that is characterized by a similar change from attentiveness to fearfulness and that has clear behavioral expression—the infant's reactions to strangers. To be sure, Rheingold and Eckerman (1973) have raised a number of questions about the universality of the phenomenon and its usefulness as a developmental landmark. Nevertheless, Sroufe, Waters, and Matas (1974) have pointed out that in certain contexts fear of strangers can be reliably elicited and adequately measured in groups of subjects, and Emde *et al.* (in press) have recently captured on film the behaviors indicative of the developmental shift that infants undergo when approached by a stranger.

Moreover, the fear of strangers paradigm can also give us finer analyses of the relation of HR to behaviorally expressed affect. For example, we would expect that the more stressful the context in which the infant was tested, the more acceleratory the cardiac response to strangers. Therefore, testing the infant in the presence and absence of the mother could give us further corroboration of our interpretation of the HR response.

Finally, the HR response could be correlated with behavioral responses to give us indications whether in given subjects behavioral ratings of facial expression, for example, were related to the HR response.

Consequently, in collaboration with Robert Emde and Ted Gaensbauer of the University of Colorado Medical School, we designed a study of the cardiac and behavioral correlates of the fear of strangers in infants 5 and 9 months of age (paralleling the ages tested in the Schwartz *et al.*, 1973, visual cliff study). Emde and Gaensbauer, together with Robert Harmon, had developed sensitive techniques of 16-mm film recording of behavioral reactions in infants and very reliable scoring categories of affect expression, which were used in the study.

The investigation involved the subject's being tested in a livingroom-like laboratory where the subject was approached by two male strangers in turn. The mother's presence and absence was counterbalanced with four orders of testing:

ORDER A: Stranger 1 enters and departs; Stranger 2 enters and departs; mother departs; mother enters.

ORDER B: Mother departs; Stranger 1 enters and departs; mother enters; Stranger 2 enters and departs.

ORDER C: Stranger 1 enters and departs; mother departs; Stranger 2 enters and departs; mother enters.

ORDER D: Mother departs; Stranger 1 enters and departs; Stranger 2 enters and departs; mother enters.

The stranger's appearance involved four 15-sec phases. In Phase 1, he entered the room and from a distance of 4 m smiled and talked to the child in a normal conversational voice (the "entry"' phase).

At a signal visible to the stranger but not to the infant, the stranger approached to within 1 m of the baby, while continuing to talk and smile (the "approach" phase).

After 15 sec, another light instructed the stranger to come very close to the infant (within .3 m), reaching out toward him and continuing to talk and smile (the "intrude" phase).

The final stage involved the stranger's receding slowly from the room, saying "bye, bye," until the 15 sec elapsed, at which time the stranger opened the entry door and exited (the "depart" phase).

For some analyses, HR and behavioral were scored every 3 sec in this study, to equate for the sampling scheme used with the two response measures. Therefore, there were five HR and behavioral responses scored within each 15-sec phase of the stranger episode. Facial activity, motor activity, direction of response, and global judgment of distress were scored by two observers, viewing the 16-mm films. At present, behavioral data are available only for facial expressions, which were scored on a six-point scale as follows: smiling, fascinated expression, sober, frown, whimper face, and cry face. Interrater reliability in categorizing these expressions was 86% for perfect agreement.

The results of the study supported in every major respect our interpretation of the cardiac response. First of all, a developmental shift was found in HR (as well as in behavior), with the 5-month-old subjects showing predominantly cardiac decelerations to the stranger and the 9-month-olds showing accelerations, on the average, especially at the points when the stranger is most intrusive or shortly thereafter (see Figures 1.6 and 1.7).

Second, the HR response to strangers was acceleratory primarily in those conditions in which the stranger approached the infant in the absence of the mother, thereby supporting our contention about the sensitivity of the HR response to the threat value of the situation. These trends are evident both in the averages of all subjects and in specific orders of testing. Figure 1.8 demonstrates how in Order A, in which both strangers approached the infant in the mother's presence, the cardiac response to the first stranger is deceleratory at both ages (except for one data point,

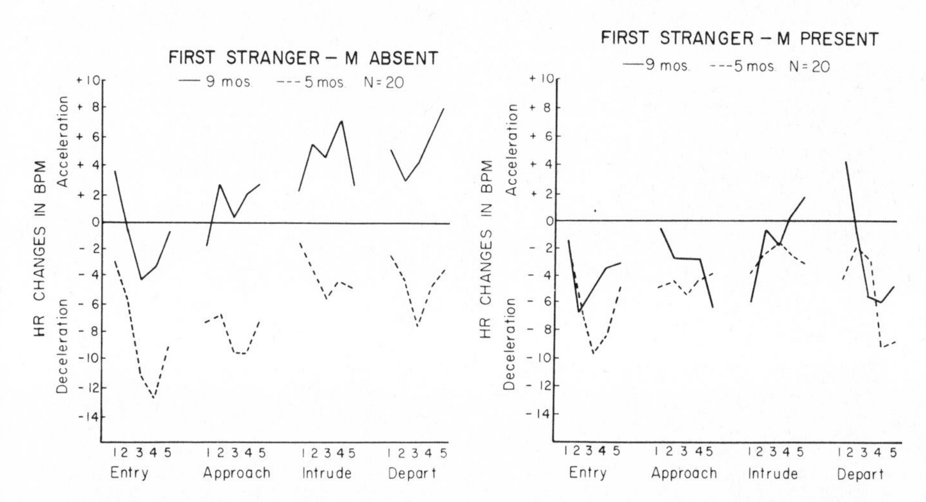

FIGURE 1.6 Cardiac responses of 5- and 9-month-old infants in response to approach and departure of a stranger. Abscissa represents 3-sec scoring intervals within each 15-sec phase of the stranger's. (Data from Campos, Emde, Gaensbauer, & Henderson, 1975.)

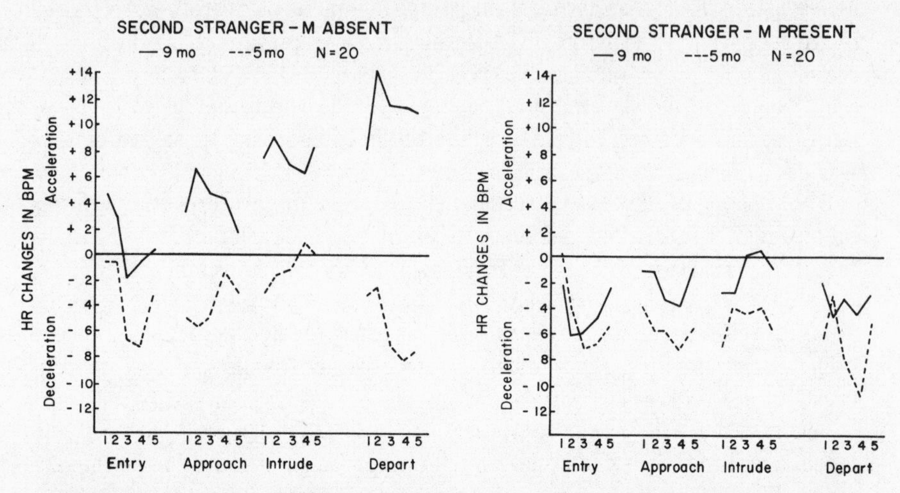

FIGURE 1.7 Cardiac responses of 5- and 9-month-old infants to approach of the second of two male strangers. (Data from Campos, Emde, Gaensbauer, & Henderson, 1975.)

which is acceleratory for the 9-month-olds). In Order D, however, in which both strangers approached the infant in the mother's absence, the 9-month-olds' responses are almost exclusively acceleratory and of very large magnitude.

Third, Figure 1.9 shows the interrelationship between cardiac responses and concomitantly measured facial expression ratings in the course of the entry, approach, intrusion, and departure phases of the study. These data were obtained from two subgroups of five subjects at each of the two ages tested. These subjects were selected because their behavioral ratings demonstrated a steady increment in distress to the stranger during the experimental sequence. With this approach, we hoped to be able to determine the extent to which HR change and facial expression ratings covaried as the distress mounted in the infant. Furthermore, we selected subjects at both the ages tested (*a*) because some 5-month-olds, as has been reported earlier (Schaffer, 1966), do show stranger distress and (*b*) to demonstrate that HR change varies with facial expression rating with age held constant.

Note in Figure 1.9 that the relationship of HR change to facial expression ratings is close. At both ages, when the subject entered the room, the subject's facial expression took on an interested appearance, and HR decelerated. The brief acceleration of Interval 1 of entry in the subgroup

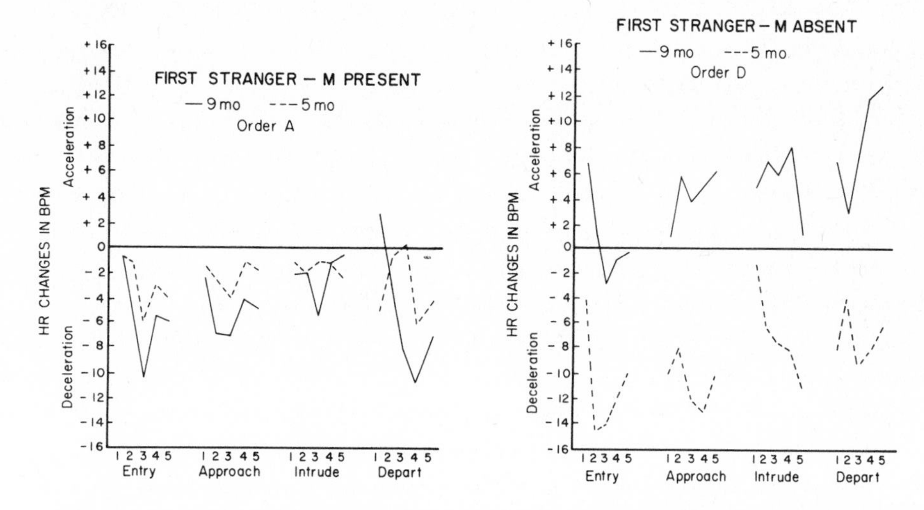

FIGURE 1.8 Cardiac responses of 5- and 9-month-old infants to approach of a male stranger in each of two testing orders: Order A, with the mother present; Order B, with the mother absent.

of 5-month-olds suggests that they may have been initially startled on the entry of the stranger. This initial phase of attentiveness to a stranger at a distance has been reported by others (e.g., Sroufe *et al.,* 1974). Subsequently, in both subgroups, as facial expression ratings become increasingly negative, HR responding tends to become less deceleratory, eventually shifting to large-magnitude accelerations (+27 BPM in the 9-month-olds). A major exception to this rule occurred in Intervals 1 and 2 of the depart phase in the 5-month subgroup, and Interval 5 of the intrude phase, and Interval 1 of the depart phase in the 9-month subgroup. (The reason for these exceptions is described shortly.)

The data obtained with these subgroups of subjects also could be used to determine whether HR responding precedes behavioral responding. Previous research (Campos & Johnson, 1966) had shown that HR could anticipate overt behavioral responding. Furthermore, because the behavioral response was not as sensitive as cardiac responding in the visual cliff situation, we had expected the HR in this situation to show changes that preceded behavioral ones. Examination of the data of individual subjects showed this to be the case for some subjects. However, for others, the behavioral response preceded the cardiac. For the modal subject, the cardiac and facial expression responses tended to covary closely in response to strangers.

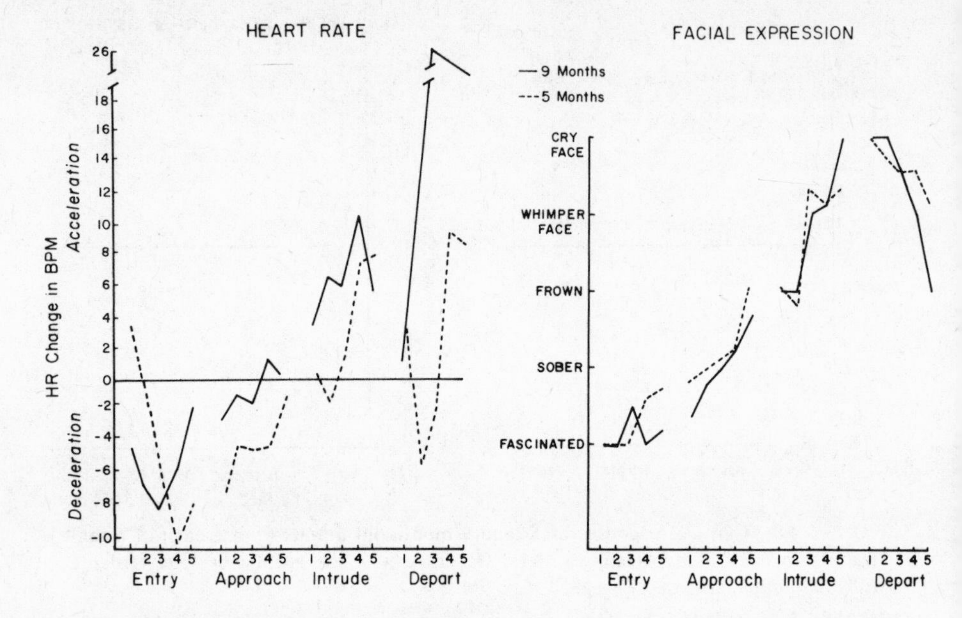

FIGURE 1.9 Concomitantly scored cardiac and facial expression responses of 5- and 9-month-old infants who first appeared to be attentive to stranger and subsequently showed facial expressions indicative of distress.

Figure 1.9 gives a hint at a feature of the HR response that may account for its frequently greater sensitivity to affective situations than behavioral responses. The HR measure has many more units within which to vary (i.e., a greater range between "floor" and "ceiling") than does the typical behavioral rating, and in the entry, intrude, and depart phases, HR response therefore seems to show more "spread" than the behavioral ones, which have approximated their limits of variation. Thus, while HR in the present study has not seemed generally to precede facial expression changes, its quantification may result in a more sensitive index of emotionality, overall, than do some other quantifications of behavioral responses.

The results of the study with strangers therefore suggest strongly a link between cardiac acceleration and fear or defensiveness. However, the cardiac response in this study on occasion showed a major exception to the trend linking HR deceleration to orienting, and acceleration to defensiveness. Typically, when an infant cried intensely and "noiselessly" (because of breath holding), the HR response, after a brief period of acceleration, showed a marked deceleration, lasting for several seconds. Figure 1.10 shows an example of such a crying-related bradycardia. In this instance, HR dropped from a high of 150 BPM to a low of 80 BPM. Although this is a stress-related deceleration, which of necessity complicates a time-sampling HR scoring scheme, we believe that the "cry drop" in HR can be readily distinguished in most cases from an attention-induced deceleration. We never observed such large-magnitude swift-decline HR decelerations during attentive episodes, no matter how rapt.

Similar periods of marked cardiac slowing are known to occur in other contexts. When an organism, such as a seal, dives into water, a marked bradycardia termed the "diving reflex" is elicited, its purpose being to conserve oxygen during a period of anoxia (Bron, Murdaugh, Millen, Lenthall,

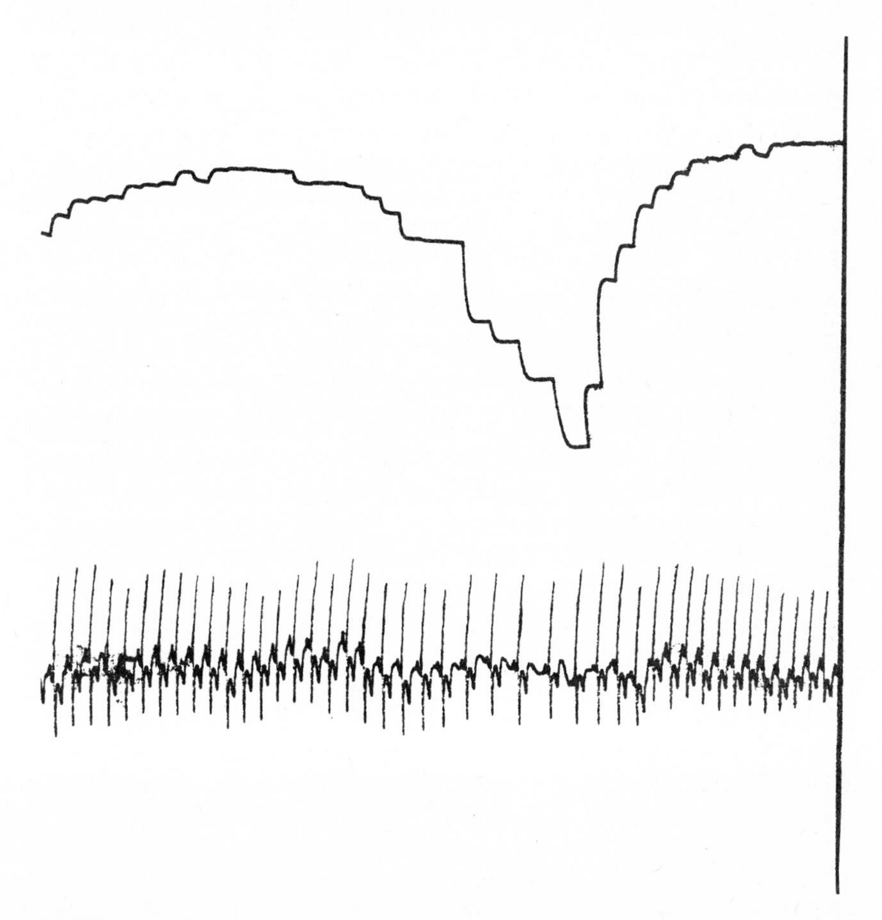

FIGURE 1.10 Cardiotachometer (upper tracing) and the electrocardiograph (lower tracing) demonstrating marked bradycardia during the breath-holding (noiseless) cry in infants.

Raskin, & Robin, 1966). Marked bradycardias can also be elicited by performance of the Valsalva maneuver, consisting of inspiration against a closed glottis. The Valsalva maneuver, reduces HR precipitously by reducing venous return to the heart (Rushmer, 1970). Although we did not have recordings of respiration, observation of the filmed records indicated that the infants in the "noiseless" crying phase were holding their breath at the peak of inspiration. Furthermore, the period of apnea was of sufficient duration that oxygen-conserving mechanisms may have been mobilized, as in the diving reflex. We interpret the crying-induced bradycardia as the intrusion of a physiological reflex into a predominantly acceleratory cardiac episode, therefore, and propose that scoring criteria be set up in future studies so that such marked slowing in one or two subjects does not bias the mean HR record in a downward direction, as has occurred in the points alluded to earlier in Figure 1.9. However, it is well to keep in mind Lacey and Lacey's (1974) dictum that the cardiac response is multidetermined. The use of HR in studies of emotional development should always be buttressed with careful recordings of ongoing behavior so as to facilitate interpretation of the HR record.

OTHER RESEARCH ON HEART RATE AND EMOTION

Other reports of cardiac acceleratory responses occurring in conditions of fear, defensiveness, or distress are beginning to accumulate. Provost and Gouin Décarie (1974) selected 9–12-month-old infants according to whether behavioral ratings showed them to be reacting aversively or positively toward strangers. The infants who were rated as reacting positively to the strangers showed large and statistically significant HR decelerations to the approach of a stranger. In contrast the infants rated as reacting negatively showed steady HR increases during the stranger's approach, reaching a peak acceleration of over 18 BPM. Similarly, Sroufe *et al.* (1974) have obtained cardiac accelerations in 10-month-old infants approached by a stranger, and significantly greater acceleration in a laboratory than in the infant's home.

Hruska and Yonas (1972) have reported finding still another developmental shift in cardiac response of human infants. They found cardiac decelerations to optically projected looming stimuli in the first 6 months of life, that shifted to accelerations by 8–10 months of age. None of the control stimuli that they used (instantaneous brightness shifts), however, elicited acceleratory responses. Although this study is similar in its implications to the studies of cardiac reactions on the visual cliff just described, they are nonetheless surprising. Previous research with dark-reared animals (Schiff, 1965) and with very young human infants (Bower,

Broughton, & Moore, 1970; Ball & Tronick, 1971) had reported that defensive behaviors were elicited by looming stimuli. Hruska and Yonas's failure to replicate these findings with HR therefore suggests the need for still another study closely investigating both HR and behavioral expression to a perceptual display.

Animal infant studies are also beginning to report cardiac accelerations in conditions of distress. In a study of infant monkeys implanted with telemetry equipment and subsequently separated from their mothers, Reite, Kaufman, Pauley, and Stynes (1974) found marked elevations in HR immediately after the separation experience, during the "agitation" phase of the infant's reaction to maternal loss.

Research with human adults presented with phobic stimuli has also demonstrated cardiac accelerations as well as verbalizations of fearfulness (Prigatano & Johnson, 1974). May and Johnson (1974) have reported obtaining markedly greater cardiac accelerations to phobic thoughts than to neutral ones in college-age subjects.

The consistency of these recent research findings linking HR accelerations with fear-provoking conditions contrasts with the findings often obtained (as mentioned earlier) in classical "fear" conditioning studies. In the absence of further evidence, it seems reasonable to categorize the classically conditioned HR deceleratory response separately from more naturalistic stressor conditions, which seem generally to elicit accelerations.

To conclude that HR acceleration is elicited in fearful or defensive situations is not to say that other HR reactions to stressful situations are not possible or have not been documented. The situations in which we and others have found cardiac acceleration in response to stress have been phasic ones, lasting no more than a few minutes (e.g., Provost & Gouin Décarie, 1974). Evidence is mounting that when certain stressful situations continue, the response can become bradycardic. Hofer (1970) in particular has documented how infant rats separated from their mothers show a tonic HR slowing of large magnitude. A similar phenomenon has been reported in infant monkeys undergoing separation: After a brief period of marked cardiac acceleration, infant monkeys show a tonic HR slowing evident during periods of both sleep and wakefulness (Reite *et al.*, 1974). The studies by Hofer and by Reite *et al.* may be measuring the cardiac correlate of depressive emotional responses. However, Anderson and Brady (1973) have reported that adult monkeys anticipating very stressful periods of Sidman avoidance (and so probably in a state of fear) show progressive HR slowing that is accompanied by increases in blood pressure. Because Anderson and Brady found HR accelerations during the actual Sidman avoidance task, it seems reasonable to conclude that the cardiac response in the immediate pressure of a fear-provoking or defensive situation is indeed an acceleration.

THE RELATIONS OF THESE RESULTS TO THE EXPLANATIONS OF DIRECTIONALITY OF HEART RATE CHANGE

On the whole, the patterns of findings in studies of cardiac acceleration and deceleration are consistent with both the Lacey hypothesis and that of Graham and Clifton. When the infant seems to be attending to the environment or orienting to a stimulus, HR decelerates; when he seems to be averting his gaze or "defending" against a stimulus, HR accelerates. The same pattern of findings could also be said to be consistent with Obrist's explanation of the nature of HR changes, because attentive situations are accompanied by apparent motoric quieting, and fearful ones by apparent increases in somatic involvement (e.g., whimpering, crying). The approaches of the Laceys and Obrist need not be mutually exclusive, but there is one major point of difference between the theories: The Laceys hold that HR activity influences cortical activity through a feedback mechanism; Obrist's theory does not. Because our studies did not address themselves to this issue (nor has any study done with infants, to our knowledge), our data remain explainable by any of these hypotheses.

DIRECTIONS FOR FUTURE RESEARCH

The studies described point to a number of important issues for future research. One significant question concerns why there should be a developmental shift in human infant reactions on the visual cliff's deep side. The issue must be phrased in the context of the human infant, because infant rhesus monkeys (Rosenblum & Cross, 1963), as well as other very young organisms (Walk & Gibson, 1961), react with fear on the deep side even in the newborn period. This is the very same question that has been asked about the developmental shift in infant reactions to strangers (Morgan & Ricciuti, 1969; Schaffer, 1966) and about the distress that infants begin to show at the mother's departure at 5 (Stayton, Ainsworth, & Main, 1973) or 7 (Schaffer & Emerson, 1964) months of age. We wonder, as did Scarr and Salapatek (1970), about whether there is similarity in the time of onset of these various fears, or whether the developmental shift occurs consistently earlier to some elicitors than to others.

Uncovering the determinants of affective development has not proved easy. Both Scarr and Salapatek (1970) and Morgan, Levin, and Harmon (1974) have reported very few significant experiential determinants of later affective development. If one is to go by recent trends in theories of emotion, one might wonder about the extent to which the shift in reactions in these emotional situations reflects the development of what

Arnold (1960), Lazarus (1968), and Pribram (1967) refer to as "appraisal." Such a viewpoint could account for the development of emotion in the absence of frequent environmental antecedents of emotion (such as falls from a bed). Some researchers (e.g., Schaffer, 1966) have suggested that the infant must develop object permanence (Piaget, 1954) as a prerequisite for fear of the stranger. Simultaneously with the development of object permanence, Piaget posits the construction of numerous spatial relationships. In the case of the visual cliff, it is possible that the construction of the relationship of above and below must occur before fear of depths is manifest. However, testing such cognitive constructs has always proved to be extremely difficult. The research evidence correlating Piagetian cognitive development with affective development has so far proved disappointing (cf. Scarr & Salapatek, 1970; Emde *et al.,* 1976, in press; Gouin Décarie, 1974). Future research may have to develop more sensitive indices of cognitive level than were available to these authors, if a relationship between cognition and affect is to emerge. A similar conclusion holds for the link between experiential antecedents and affective expression. We must look harder for currently unexplored experiential antecedents of affect.

A number of authors, such as Freedman (1965) and Emde *et al.* (1976, in press), have argued that these developmental shifts reflect maturational–hereditary processes that affect the development of emotion in the first year of life. Freedman has shown how there is considerable similarity in the time of onset of various emotional responses in identical twins. The possibility that maturational factors may be playing a role must not be overlooked, but it seems conceptually difficult to separate the hereditary–maturational component from that of cognitive or experiential influences. It is possible that there is a degree of similarity of intellectual development in human identical twins (e.g., Freedman & Keller, 1963; Wilson, 1972) that, through the mediation of similar appraisals, can then account for similarity in emotional expression. It is also possible that maturation merely primes the organism to form associations which are not easily formed at an earlier age and for which the requisite experience is still necessary (cf. Seligman, 1970).

However the determinants of fear development are conceptualized, it seems reasonable to propose that HR responses may be a sensitive and reliable index with which to probe for affective shifts in infancy. We have already alluded to the importance of research with optical expansion patterns. The potential significance of the HR response can be extended in several directions, as well. For example, it may be worthwhile to investigate the infant's HR response as an attachment behavior. Many of the attachment behaviors shown by prelocomotor infants (e.g., crying) are not differential to the mother until late in the first year of life (e.g., Fleener

& Cairns, 1970). Although Stayton *et al.* (1973) have reported differential crying to the mother and a stranger in the second quarter year of life, the percentage of subjects showing this differentiality is small. More significant results may emerge through the use of HR.

Several other emotions might be fruitfully indexed with HR. Bower (1971), for example, found HR to be sensitive to manipulations that induced surprise in young infants of various ages. The interesting finding in animals of marked bradycardia, cited earlier, may illuminate the psychophysiology of infant depression following maternal loss (such as still occurs in humans, unfortunately, after late adoptions, divorce, or maternal death). Laughter and smiling are still other emotional responses that may yield interesting relationships with HR.

For years, psychologists have postulated physiological activation as one of the defining criteria of emotion. Although none of the research we have discussed suggests that HR change is specific to any given emotion, or to emotions in general, it seems clear that under certain circumstances the sensitivity of the HR response under emotionally stimulating circumstances has been demonstrated. It remains for future research to document the applications and limitations of this response. Nevertheless, it seems a fair conclusion at this time to suggest the addition of cardiac response measurement to the tools of the student of infant emotion.

ACKNOWLEDGMENTS

This research has been supported by grants MH 19053 and MH 23556 from the National Institutes of Mental Health, by Training Grant MH 08297, and by faculty research funds awarded by the Graduate School of Arts and Sciences, University of Denver.

REFERENCES

Ainsworth, M. Patterns of attachment behavior shown by the infant in interaction with his mother. *Merrill-Palmer Quarterly,* 1964, **10,** 51–58.

Anders, T., Emde, R., & Parmelee, A. *A manual of standardized terminology, techniques and criteria for scoring of states of sleep and wakefulness in newborn infants.* Los Angeles: UCLA Brain Information Service, 1971.

Anderson, D., & Brady, J. V. Prolonged preavoidance effects upon blood pressure and heart rate in the dog. *Psychosomatic Medicine,* 1973, **35,** 4–12.

Apgar, V. A proposal for a new method of evaluation of the newborn infant. *Current Research in Anesthesia and Analgesia,* 1953, **32,** 260–267.

Appel, M. Binocular parallax in the human infant. Unpublished doctoral dissertation. University of Denver, Denver, Colorado, 1971.

Arnold, M. *Emotion and personality.* New York: Columbia University Press, 1960. Vols. I and II.

Ball, W., & Tronick, E. Infant responses to impending collision: Optical and real. *Science,* 1971, **171,** 818–820.

Bartoshuk, A. Human neonatal cardiac responses to sound: A power function. *Psychonomic Science,* 1964, **1,** 151–152.

Bersh, P. J., Notterman, J. M., & Schoenfeld, W. N. Extinction of human cardiac response during avoidance conditioning. *American Journal of Psychology,* 1956, **69,** 244–251.

Birns, B., Blank, M., & Bridger, W. H. The effectiveness of various soothing techniques on human neonates. *Psychosomatic Medicine,* 1966, **28,** 316–322.

Bonvallet, M., & Allen, M. B. Prolonged spontaneous and evoked reticular activation following discrete bulbar lesions. *Electroencephalography and Clinical Neurophysiology,* 1963, **15,** 969–988.

Bonvallet, M., & Bloch, V. Bulbar control of cortical arousal. *Science,* 1961, **133,** 1133–1134.

Bower, T. Depth perception in the premotor human infant. *Psychonomic Science,* 1964, **1,** 365.

Bower, T. Stimulus variables determining space perception in infants. *Science,* 1965, **149,** 88–89.

Bower, T. Slant perception and shape constancy in infants. *Science,* 1966, **151,** 832–834.

Bower, T. The object in the world of the infant. *Scientific American,* 1971, **225**(4), 30–38.

Bower, T., Broughton, M., & Moore, K. Infant responses to approaching objects: An indicator of response to distal variables. *Perception & Psychophysics,* 1970, **9,** 193–195.

Brackbill, Y. Cumulative effects of continuous stimulation on arousal level in infants. *Child Development,* 1971, **42,** 17–26.

Bridger, W. H. Sensory habituation and discrimination in the human neonate. *American Journal of Psychiatry,* 1961, **117,** 991–996.

Bridger, W. H., Birns, B. M., & Blank, M. A comparison of behavioral ratings and heart rate measurements in human neonates. *Psychosomatic Medicine,* 1965, **27,** 123–134.

Bridger, W. H., & Reiser, M. F. Psychophysiological studies of the neonate: An approach toward the methodological and theoretical problems involved. *Psychosomatic Medicine,* 1959, **21,** 265–276.

Bron, K. M., Murdaugh, H. V., Millen, E., Lenthall, R., Raskin, P., & Robin, E. Arterial constrictor response in a diving mammal. *Science,* 1966, **152,** 541–543.

Campos, J. J., & Brackbill, Y. Infant state: Relationship to heart rate, behavioral response and response decrement. *Development Psychobiology,* 1973, **6,** 9–19.

Campos, J. J., Emde, R., Gaensbauer, T., & Henderson, C. Cardiac and behavioral interrelationships in the reactions of infants to strangers. *Developmental Psychology,* 1975, **11,** 589–601.

Campos, J. J., & Johnson, H. J. The effects of verbalization instructions and visual attention on heart rate and skin conductance. *Psychophysiology,* 1966, **2,** 305–310.

Campos, J. J., & Langer, A. The visual cliff: Discriminative cardiac orienting responses with retinal size held constant. Paper read at the meetings of the Society for Psychophysiological Research, 1970. *Psychophysiology,* 1971, **8,** 264–265. (Abstract)

Campos, J. J., Langer, A., & Krowitz, A. Cardiac responses on the visual cliff in prelocomotor human infants. *Science,* 1970, **170,** 195–196.

Campos, J. J., Tursky, B., & Conway, E. Skin potential and skin resistance responses of the very young human infant. Paper read at the meetings of the Society for

Psychophysiological Research, 1970. *Psychophysiology,* 1971, **8,** 253–254. (Abstract)
Cannon, W. B. The James–Lange theory of emotions: A critical examination and an alternative theory. *American Journal of Psychology,* 1927, **39,** 106–124.
Clifton, R. K., & Graham, F. K. Stability of individual differences in heart rate activity during the newborn period. *Psychophysiology,* 1968, **5,** 37–50.
Conway, E. Effects of stimulus intensity upon the physiological responding of young infants. Unpublished doctoral dissertation, University of Denver, Denver, Colorado, 1972.
Crowell, D., Davis, C., Chun, B., & Spellacy, F. Galvanic skin reflex in newborn humans. *Science,* 1965, **148,** 1108–1111.
Duffy, E. *Activation and behavior.* New York: Wiley, 1962.
Ellingson, R. J. Cortical electrical responses to visual stimulation in the human infant. *Electroencephalography and Clinical Neurophysiology,* 1960, **12,** 663–677.
Elliot, R. The significane of heart rate for behavior: A critique of Lacey's hypothesis. *Journal of Personality and Social Psychology,* 1972, **22,** 398–409.
Emde, R. N., Gaensbauer, T. J., & Harmon, R. J. Emotional expression in infancy: A biobehavioral study. *Psychological Issues,* 1976, in press.
Emde, R. N., & Metcalf, D. R. An electroencephalographic study of behavioral rapid eye movement states in the human newborn. *Journal of Nervous and Mental Diseases,* 1970, **150,** 376–386.
Fleener, D., & Cairns, R. Attachment behaviors in human infants: Discriminative vocalization on maternal separation. *Developmental Psychology,* 1970, **2,** 215–223.
Fitzgerald, H. E. Autonomic pupillary reflex activity during early infancy and its relation to social and nonsocial visual stimuli. *Journal of Experimental Child Psychology,* 1968, **6,** 470–482.
Freedman, D. G. An ethological approach to the genetical study of human behavior. In S. Vandenberg (Ed.), *Methods and goals in human behavior genetics.* New York: Academic Press, 1965. Pp. 1–7.
Freedman, D. G., & Keller, B. Inheritance of behavior in infants. *Science,* 1963, **140,** 196–198.
Gibson, E., & Walk, R. The "visual cliff." *Scientific American,* 1960, **202,** 64–71.
Gouin Décarie, T. *The infant's reactions to strangers.* New York: International Universities Press, 1974.
Graham, F. K., Berg, K., Berg, K., Jackson, J., Hatton, H., & Kantowitz, S. Cardiac orienting responses as a function of age. *Psychonomic Science,* 1970, **19,** 363–365.
Graham, F. K., & Clifton, R. Heart-rate change as a component of the orienting response. *Psychological Bulletin,* 1966, **65,** 305–320.
Graham, F. K., & Jackson, J. C. Arousal systems and infant heart rate responses. In H. W. Reese & L. P. Lipsitt (Eds.), *Advances in child development and behavior.* Vol. 5. New York: Academic Press, 1970. Pp. 59–117.
Hahn, W. W. Attention and heart rate: A critical appraisal of the hypothesis of Lacey and Lacey. *Psychological Bulletin,* 1973, **79,** 59–70.
Haynes, H., White, B. L., & Held, R. Visual accommodation in human infants. *Science,* 1965, **148,** 528–530.
Hofer, M. A. Physiological responses of infant rats to separation from their mothers. *Science,* 1970, **168,** 871–873.
Hon, E. H. Observation on "pathogenic" fetal bradycardia. *American Journal of Obstetrics and Gynecology,* 1959, **77,** 1084.
Horowitz, A. B. Habituation and memory: Infant cardiac responses to familiar and discrepant auditory stimuli. *Child Development,* 1972, **43,** 43–54.
House, B. J., & Zeaman, D. Minature experiments in the discrimination learning

of retardates. In L. P. Lipsitt & C. C. Spiker (Eds.), *Advances in child development and behavior*. Vol. 1. New York: Academic Press, 1963.

Hruska, K., & Yonas, A. Developmental changes in cardiac responses to the optical stimulus of impending collision. Paper read at the Meetings of the Society for Psychophysiological Research, St. Louis, Missouri, October 1971. *Psychophysiology*, 1972, **9,** 272. (Abstract)

Kagan, J. On cultural deprivation. In D. Glass (Ed.), *Environmental influences.* New York: Rockefeller University Press, 1968. Pp. 211–250.

Kagan, J., & Lewis, M. Studies of attention in the human infant. *Merrill-Palmer Quarterly,* 1965, **11,** 95–127.

Karmel, B. Z. Complexity, amount of contour, and visually dependent preference behavior in hooded rats, domestic chicks, and human infants. *Journal of Comparative and Physiological Psychology,* 1969, **69,** 649–657.

Kearsley, R. B. The newborn's response to auditory stimulation: A demonstration of orienting and defensive behavior. *Child Development,* 1973, **44,** 582–590.

Lacey, J. I., Kagan, J., Lacey, B., & Moss, H. The visceral level: Situational determinants and behavioral correlates of autonomic response patterns. In P. H. Knapp (Ed.), *Expression of the emotions in man.* New York: International Universities Press, 1963. Pp. 161–196.

Lacey, J. I., & Lacey, B. The relationship of resting autonomic activity to motor impulsivity. *Research Publications Association for Research in Nervous and Mental Disease,* 1958, **36,** 144–209.

Lacey, J. I., & Lacey, B. C. Some autonomic–central nervous system interrelationships. In P. Black (Ed.), *Physiological correlates of emotion.* New York: Academic Press, 1970. Pp. 205–228.

Lacey, J. I., & Lacey, B. C. On heart rate responses and behavior: A reply to Elliott. *Journal of Personality and Social Psychology,* 1974, **30,** 1–18.

Lazarus, R. Emotions and adaptations: Conceptual and empirical relations. In W. Arnold (Ed.), *Nebraska symposium on motivation.* Vol. 16. Lincoln: University of Nebraska Press, 1968. Pp. 175–270.

Lewis, M. A developmental study of the cardiac response to stimulus onset and offset during the first year of life. *Psychophysiology,* 1971, **8,** 689–698.

Lewis, M., & Goldberg, S. The acquisition and violation of an expectancy: An experimental paradigm. *Journal of Experimental Child Psychology,* 1969, **7,** 70–80.

Lewis, M., Kagan, J., Campbell, H., & Kalafat, J. The cardiac response as a correlate of attention in infants. *Child Development,* 1966, **37,** 63–71.

Lewis, M., & Spaulding, S. J. Differential cardiac response to visual and auditory stimulation in the young child. *Psychophysiology,* 1967, **3,** 229–238.

Lindsley, D. B. Emotion. In S. S. Stevens, (Ed.), *Handbook of experimental psychology.* New York: Wiley, 1951. Pp. 473–516.

Lipsitt, L. P., & Jacklin, C. N. Cardiac deceleration and its stability in human newborns. *Developmental Psychology,* 1971, **5,** 535.

Lipton, E. L., Steinschneider, A., & Richmond, J. B. The autonomic nervous system in early life. *New England Journal of Medicine,* 1965, **273,** 147–153.

Lipton, E. L., Steinschneider, A., & Richmond, J. B. Autonomic function in the neonate: VII. Maturational changes in cardiac control. *Child Development,* 1966, **37,** 1–16.

Lynn, R. *Attention, arousal and the orientation reaction.* New York: Pergamon Press, 1966.

Malmo, R. B. Activation: A neurophysiological dimension. *Psychological Review,* 1959, **66,** 367–386.

May, J., & Johnson, H. J. Peripheral physiological activity to internally elicited phobic and non-phobic thoughts. Paper read at the Meetings of the Society for Psychophysiological Research, Galveston, Texas, October 1973. *Psychophysiology,* 1974, **11,** 229. (Abstract)

Merryweather, J., Campos, J., Schwartz, M., & Flanders, P. Twenty-four hour retention of an habituated heart rate response in three and a half month old infants. Paper read at the meetings of the Society for Research in Child Development, Philadelphia, Pennsylvania, 1973.

Morgan, G. A., Levin, B., & Harmon, R. Determinants of individual differences in infant's reactions to unfamiliar adults. Paper presented at the Southeastern Conference of the Society for Research in Child Development, Chapel Hill, North Carolina, March, 1974.

Morgan, G. A., & Ricciuti, H. Infant's responses to strangers during the first year. In B. M. Foss (Ed.), *Determinants of infant behavior*. London: Methuen, 1969. Pp. 253–272.

Mowrer, O. H. *Learning theory and behavior*. New York: Wiley, 1960.

Obrist, P. A. Cardiovascular differentiation of sensory stimuli. *Psychosomatic Medicine,* 1963, **25,** 450–459.

Obrist, P. A., Webb, R. A., Sutterer, J. R., & Howard, J. L. The cardiac–somatic relationship: Some reformulations. *Psychophysiology,* 1970, **6,** 569–587.

Obrist, P. A., Wood, D. M., & Perez-Reyes, M. Heart rate during conditioning in humans: Effect of UCS intensity, vagal blockade, and adrenergic block of vasomotor activity. *Journal of Experimental Psychology,* 1965, 70, 32–42.

Piaget, J. *The origins of intelligence*. New York: Basic Books, 1951.

Piaget, J. *The construction of reality in the child*. New York: Basic Books, 1954.

Porges, S. W. Heart rate indices of newborn attentional responsivity. *Merrill-Palmer Quarterly,* 1974, **20,** 231–254.

Porges, S. W., Arnold, W. R., & Forbes, E. J. Heart rate variability: An index of attentional responsivity in human newborns. *Developmental Psychology,* 1973, **8,** 85–92.

Pribram, K. Emotion: Steps toward a neuropsychological theory. In D. Glass (Ed.), *Neurophysiology and emotion*. New York: Rockefeller University Press, 1967. Pp. 3–40.

Prigatano, G. P., & Johnson, H. J. ANS changes associated with spider phobic reaction. *Journal of Abnormal Psychology,* 1974, **83,** 169–177.

Provost, M., & Gouin Décarie, T. Modifications du rhythme cardiaque chez des enfants de 9–12 mois au cours de la recontre avec la personne étrangère. *Canadian Journal of Behavioral Science,* 1974, **6,** 154–168.

Rechtschaffen, A., & Kales, A. *A manual of standardized terminology, techniques, and scoring system for sleep stages of human subjects*. Washington, D.C.: U.S. Government Printing Office, 1968.

Reite, M., Kaufman, I. C., Pauley, J. D., & Stynes, A. J. Depression in infant monkeys: Physiological correlates. *Psychosomatic Medicine,* 1974, **36,** 363–367.

Rheingold, H., & Eckerman, C. Fear of the stranger: A critical examination. In H. Reese (Ed.), *Advances in child development and behavior*. Vol. 8. New York: Academic Press, 1973. Pp. 185–222.

Rosenblum, L., & Cross, H. Performance of neonatal monkeys in the visual cliff situation. *American Journal of Psychology,* 1963, **76,** 318–320.

Rushmer, R. F. *Cardiovascular dynamics*. Philadelphia: W. B. Saunders, 1970.

Sameroff, A. J., Cashmore, T. F., & Dykes, A. C. Heart rate deceleration during visual fixation in human newborns. *Developmental Psychology,* 1973, **8,** 117–119.

Scarr, S., & Salapatek, P. Patterns of fear development during infancy. *Merrill-Palmer Quarterly,* 1970, **16,** 53–90.

Schaffer, H. R. The onset of fear of strangers and the incongruity hypothesis. *Journal of Child Psychology and Psychiatry,* 1966, **7,** 95–106.

Schaffer, H., & Emerson, P. The development of social attachments in infancy. *Monographs of the Society for Research in Child Development,* 1964, **29** (Serial No. 94).

Schiff, W. Perception of impending collision: A study of visually directed avoidant behavior. *Psychological Monographs,* 1965, **79** (11, Whole No. 604).

Schwartz, A., Campos, J., & Baisel, E. The visual cliff: Cardiac and behavioral correlates on the deep and shallow sides at five and nine months of age. *Journal of Experimental Child Psychology,* 1973, **15,** 86–99.

Seligman, M. On the generality of the laws of learning. *Psychological Review,* 1970, **77,** 406–418.

Silverman, S. Z., & Campos, J. J. Operant HR conditioning in the infant and young child. Paper read at the Meetings of the Society for Psychophysiological Research, Boston, Massachusetts, November 1972. *Psychophysiology,* 1973, **10,** 194. (Abstract)

Sokolov, E. *Perception and the conditioned reflex.* New York: Macmillan, 1963.

Sroufe, L. A., Waters, E., & Matas, L. Contexual determinants of infant affective response. In M. Lewis & L. Rosenblum (Eds.), *The origins of fear.* New York: John Wiley, 1974. Pp. 49–72.

Stayton, D., Ainsworth, M., & Main, M. Development of separation behavior in the first year of life: Protest, following and greeting. *Developmental Psychology,* 1973, **9,** 213–225.

Stechler, G., Bradford, S., & Levy, H. Attention in the newborn: Effect on motility and skin potential. *Science,* 1966, **151,** 1247–1248.

Steinschneider, A., Lipton, E. L., & Richmond, J. B. Auditory sensitivity in the infant: Effect of intensity on cardiac and motor responsivity. *Child Development,* 1966, **37,** 233–252.

Stratton, P. M., & Connolly, K. Discrimination by newborns of the intensity, frequency, and temporal characteristics of auditory stimuli. *British Journal of Psychology,* 1973, **64,** 219–232.

Tennes, K., & Carter, D. Plasma cortisol levels and behavioral states in early infancy. *Psychosomatic Medicine,* 1973, **35,** 121–128.

Walk, R., & Gibson, E. A comparative and analytical study of visual depth perception. *Psychological Monographs,* 1961, **75** (15, Whole No. 519).

Wilson, R. S. Twins: Early mental development. *Science,* 1972, **175,** 914–916.

Comments on "Heart Rate: A Sensitive Tool for the Study of Emotional Development in the Infant"

Sandra Scarr-Salapatek

Is heart rate a better mousetrap for capturing emotional status in infancy? Campos' chapter convinces me, with an impressive array of evidence, that it can serve as an index for orienting and arousal, perhaps a more sensitive one than behavioral observation. His logic is that (1) behavioral evidence of affective arousal correlates with heart rate (HR) changes; (2) HR changes are more sensitive to emotional states than behavioral measures are; therefore (3) HR may be a better measure of subtle developmental shifts and changes in state than other psychophysiological and behavioral measures.

He is careful to note, however, the shortcomings of the HR measure: It responds to internal and external stimuli other than emotional state; it does not give information about the specific emotion aroused; and it tells us nothing about the psychological processes that accompany orienting or arousal. In short, HR is a measure at the physiological, not the psychological, level.

Emotional states during infancy—and at all other ages—involve responses at both psychological and physiological levels. As psychologists, we are presumably more interested in the cognitive and behavioral aspects of emotional development than in the physiological ones per se. To the extent that HR provides information about the psychological meaning of emotional states, it is a useful tool in the study of emotional development. If HR only provides information about the physiological level of response in emotionally arousing conditions, then I contend that we should be no more interested in HR than in, say, the digestive process. Understanding obesity may involve understanding digestion, but digestion is unlikely to provide a full explanation of compulsive eating. Similarly, understanding arousal mechanisms may be important for understanding emotions in infancy, but HR can never provide a full explanation (nor does Campos claim it can). Although the difference in level of explanation does not disqualify HR as an index of emotional development, its usefulness is necessarily tied to other measures at a psychological level.

Many investigations of infant development have used behavioral responses to index emotional reactions. Facial expressions in greeting situations (Vaughn, 1974), "surprise" reactions (Charlesworth, 1969), motor avoidance (e.g., Gibson & Walk, 1960), frowning and crying (e.g., Scarr & Salapatek, 1970), and smiling and laughter (Sroufe, Waters, & Matas, 1974) have all received some attention during infancy. (Because infants cannot "tell" us in other ways about their emotional states, behavioral observations have been the best method available.) The fact that HR correlates with behavioral responses is a convenience for the experimenter, especially if an infant's behavioral responses are ambiguous.

The gain from HR recording for studying emotional development depends on its consistently high correlation with behavioral measures and the ability of the investigator to exclude other causes of HR change. When behavioral evidence is ambiguous, such as when a 7-month-old stares into the deep side of a visual cliff without moving, HR can rescue the observation. Is he fearful (HR acceleration) or merely interested in the visual display (HR deceleration)? The inference to his emotional state depends on strong evidence that given HR changes accompany unambiguous behavioral responses for other infants in this situation and in other situations. Campos presents a convincing demonstration of the consistently close relationship between HR changes and facial expressions from fascination to crying (see Figure 1.10) and the correlation of HR changes with other behavioral evidence of fear.

What information do we lose by focusing our experimental attention on HR alone? First, HR accelerations occur with both laughter and crying, responses that have quite different psychological meanings. Furthermore, the HR decelerations that occur in a 3-month-old at the "magical" disappearance of an object (violating physical laws) probably accompanies very different cognitive processes from the decelerations of a 12-month-old, who better understands the permanence of objects. If we were to record HR alone, we would lose touch with the psychological aspects of emotional development.

HR cannot be used alone to chart new territory in emotional development, because its validity as an index of emotion depends on known behavioral correlates. Suppose a 12-month-old sees his mother crawling around on the floor barking like a dog—an uncharacteristic maternal behavior prompted by a devilish experimenter. His HR first decelerates and then accelerates rapidly. What was the baby's emotional response? We would have to observe whether he laughed or cried. We do know from the HR record and its correlates in other situations that he oriented at first and then became aroused, but we know nothing about the content of his response nor why he responded as he did. To study new emotional situations and behavioral responses, HR changes will not stand alone. Behavioral observations remain the anchor for a psychological interpretation.

Individual differences in HR responses are another problem. Stable patterns of individual responses are not well established, as Campos notes, although the test–retest correlations are above zero. Because behavioral, emotional responses are not perfectly measured either (Scarr & Salapatek, 1970), there are compound problems with an unstable index of unstable criterion measures. This criticism is not directed toward HR alone; most experimental measures are not highly reliable. For the purposes of seeking age-related changes in HR responses, a moderately reliable measure will probably do. It would be more difficult, however, to explore individual differences in HR changes longitudinally.

None of the criticisms above points in any sense to a fatal flaw. They are intended as warnings about the problems of reductionist measures that lack perfect correlations with the behavioral criteria, that are not perfectly reliable, and that do not convey all of the necessary information about emotional development. Campos never made any such claims. Instead, he demonstrated in fascinating ways that HR can be a useful measure to accompany behavioral observations. Not all claims for psychophysiology are so circumspect.

REFERENCES

Charlesworth, W. R. The role of surprise in cognitive development. In D. Elkind & J. H. Flavell (Eds.), *Studies in cognitive development*. New York: Oxford University Press, 1969. Pp. 257–314.

Gibson, E., & Walk, R. The "visual cliff." *Scientific American,* 1960, **202,** 64–71.

Scarr, S., & Salapatek, P. Patterns of fear development during infancy. *Merrill-Palmer Quarterly,* 1970, **16,** 53–90.

Sroufe, L. A., Waters, E., & Matas, L. Contextual determinants of infant affective response. In M. Lewis & L. Rosenblum (Eds.), *Origins of fear*. New York: Wiley, 1974. Pp. 49–72.

Vaughn, B. The ontogeny of facial expressions used in greeting others. Unpublished manuscript, University of Minnesota, 1974.

2

Infancy, Biology, and Culture

Daniel G. Freedman

The Committee on Human Development
The University of Chicago

The thesis here is very simple minded. It is merely an extension of the monistic position in the mind–body controversy and seeks to emphasize the point that everything that man does, at some level of analysis, is reflective of his biological makeup.

Dualistic positions usually emphasize the opposition of learning and biology, so let us start by asking what we mean by learned behavior. Language provides a convenient paradigm. How is it that little children learn that sounds stand for something concrete (nouns) or actions (verbs), or, later, that they can modify the first two categories? Imitation is not the answer, for parrots can imitate but they never use language. Children somehow attach sounds to things and to actions naturally, picking up the sounds and designates of the caretakers with extraordinary skill. Even though we cannot now know what they are, biological structures must be posed as accounting for this ability. An entire school of developmental linguistics has arisen around this simple point and, as most know, the work of Chomsky (1965) on how meaning is derived from language has become the focus of a biologically based linguistic theory.

Incidentally, the fact that chimps and gorillas can be taught deaf sign language and that they can communicate it with facility is another sign of their evolutionary proximity to man. Although they never master human grammatical usage, as does even the youngest speaking human child (McNeill, 1970), no other animal has come close to their manlike communicative skills.

Although the language of communication is learned in man and chimps, therefore, the nature and limitations of what is learned is clearly biologically based. In other words, it is a logical fallacy to oppose learning with biology, because learning is completely dependent on biological structures. This holds for all learning in all species, and learning is always species specific and species dependent.

GENOTYPIC VARIATION AND HUMAN CULTURAL DIFFERENCES

Man-made culture involves the species-specific ability to abstract—to take distance on phenomena and to make known one's ideas through some means of communication, usually vocal language, and to do this in terms of planning for the future and taking cognizance of the past (Goldstein, 1963). Not even the famous chimp Washoe, who was taught deaf sign language, can use symbols in this way (McNeill, 1970). Is not this ability to abstract and to plan sufficient explanation to state that man has invented the plethora of cultural differences found in the world today? Certainly the conscious decisions of councils and chiefs must have played such a role, but just as certainly nonconscious processes have also been at work.

For one thing, it is likely that within-species genetic variation has played a role in creating cultural differences via "founder principle." Let us take a hypothetical example. Suppose there are two Polynesian islands, several hundred miles from each other, each populated by groups of 500 persons with several islands similarly populated within this several hundred mile expanse. On Island A, the people are friendly and outgoing; on Island B, they are shy and retiring. Let us suppose the founding populations of each island were single families and that friendliness or shyness differentially characterized these two families. Let us suppose further that these characteristics were at least partially based on inherited temperamental differences, an assumption for which there is now considerable evidence. It is not difficult to imagine that those Polynesian institutions which are conceivably affected by temperamental differences (e.g., public ceremonies) may take on a unique cast on each island. It seems highly likely, in fact, that it is such processes which help give rise to new cultural forms.

As we have introduced the potential role of genetic inbreeding, let us carry it forward. One implication of this reasoning is that the culture developed by an isolated group is particularly adjusted to the gene pool of that group; that is to say, the culture developed by any homogeneous people must reflect the unique biology of that people—as, for example, its temperament.

However, one may ask, how good is the evidence on the relationship between genetics and behavior? Data in this area is relatively recent, but it may now be described as vast (e.g., Hirsch, 1967; Fuller & Thompson, 1960). Let it suffice to say that in both human and animal behavior genetics, just about any trait may be shown to have a "heritable" component. According to trends in current research, therefore, if we project an infinite number of twins, an infinite number of traits should prove heritable (Freedman, 1974).

This all seems eminently logical, particularly if one starts with a monistic view of mind and body. However, it is one thing to concede that differences in behavior between individuals in part result from differences in genotype, and apparently quite another to concede that differences in behavior between human groups in part result from differences in gene pools. Yet for zoologists and botanists, within-group genetic differences go hand in glove with between-group genetic differences; both always occur in nature. Is it possible that the hominids are an exception? Certainly we are far more inbred than one would naively believe. Consider that each of us had two parents, who also each had two parents, etc. Going back but 1,000 years, and allowing four generations each century, one's own progenitors would be more than enough to populate the entire world of that time (2^{40}, or a million million, ancestors). Clearly, human groups are enormously inbred.

With this sort of logic in mind, my wife and I embarked on a series of studies of newborns of various ethnic groups. We chose newborns because one can reasonably assume they are as yet free of the social molding everyone goes through in attaining membership to a society.

One first study compared second through fourth generation newborns of Chinese and European backgrounds. Twenty-four Chinese–American and 24 European–American newborns were examined while still in the nursery. The Orientals were largely of Cantonese background and the Caucasians largely of middle-European background. All families were middle class and the bulk were members of a prepaid health plan, and the infants were matched on every potentially important covariable (age, age of mother, sibling order, weight, length of labor, etc.).

The behavior scales (Cambridge Neonatal Scales, Brazelton & Freedman, 1971) consisted of 28 general behavioral items rated 1–9 and 18 standard neurological signs, frequently used to screen for neural damage, rated 0–3. The 25 general items may be somewhat arbitrarily arranged into five categories as follows: (1) temperament, five items; (2) sensory development, three items; (3) autonomic and central nervous system maturity, eight items; (4) motor development, six items; (5) social interest and response, six items. As will be seen, any single item may overlap categories (e.g., lability of skin color can reflect temperament as well as autonomic maturity).

On the basis of total performance, the two groups were decidedly different; the main source of difference was the group of items measuring temperament, particularly those which seemed to tap excitability–imperturability. Although the following discussion is based on mean ethnic difference on the distinguishing items, it should be emphasized that there was substantial overlap in range on all scales between the Chinese and Caucasian infants.

The European–American infants reached a peak of excitement sooner (rapidity of buildup) and had a greater tendency to move back and forth between states of contentment and upset (lability of states). They showed more facial and bodily reddening probably as a consequence. The Chinese–American infants were scored on the calmer and steadier side of these items. In an item called *defensive movements,* the tester placed a cloth firmly over the supine baby's face for a few seconds. Whereas the typical European–American infant immediately struggled to remove the cloth by swiping with hands and turning his face, the typical Chinese–American infant lay impassively, exhibiting few overt motor responses. Similarly, when placed in the prone position, the Chinese infants frequently lay as placed, with face flat against the bedding, whereas the Caucasian infants either turned the face to one side or lifted the head. Inasmuch as there was no difference between the groups in the ability to hold the head steady in the upright (pull-to-sit) position, this maintenance of the face in the bedding is taken as a further example of relative imperturbability, or ready accomodation to external changes. In an apparently related item, rate of habituation, a pen light was repeatedly shone on the infant's eyes and the number of blinks was counted until the infant no longer reacted. The Chinese infants tended to habituate more readily.

There was no significant difference in amount of crying and, when picked up and consoled both groups tended to stop crying. The Chinese infants, however, were often dramatically immediate in their cessation of crying when picked up and spoken to and therefore drew extremely high ratings in consolability. The Chinese infants also tended to stop crying sooner without soothing (self-quieting ability).

To summarize, the majority of items that differentiated the two groups fell into the category of temperament. The Chinese–American newborns tended to be less changeable, and less perturbable, tended to habituate more readily, and tended to calm themselves or to be consoled more readily when upset. In other areas (sensory development, central nervous system maturity, motor development, social responsivity), the two groups were indistinguishable.

There is some evidence that similar differences characterize these two ethnic groups at later ages as well, although the data are far from conclusive. Green's (1969) study of nursery schoolers in Chicago provides evidence for similar temperamental differences at 3 and 4 years of age. The study, which was an attempt to compare children's use of space in a Chinese–American and European–American nursery school, concluded that European–American children spent significantly more time in approach and interaction behavior and that Chinese–American children spent more time concentrating on individual projects. More revealing than her quantitative findings, however, are her comments:

> Although the majority of the Chinese–American children were in the "high arousal age," between 3 and 5, they showed little intense emotional behavior. They ran and hopped, laughed and called to one another, rode bikes and roller-skated just as the children did in the other nursery schools, but the noise level stayed remarkably low and the emotional atmosphere projected serenity instead of bedlam. The impassive facial expression certainly gave the children an air of dignity and self-possession, but this was only one element effecting the total impression. Physical movements seemed more coordinated, no tripping, falling, bumping or bruising was observed, no screams, crashes or wailing was heard, not even that common sound in other nurseries, voices raised in highly indignant moralistic dispute! No property disputes were observed and only the mildest version of "fighting behavior," some good-natured wrestling among the older boys. The adults evidently had different expectations about hostile or impulsive behavior; this was the only nursery school where it was observed that children were trusted to duel with sticks. Personal distance spacing seemed to be situational rather than compulsive or patterned, and the children appeared to make no effort to avoid physical contact [Green, 1969, p. 6].

It is common observation in the public schools of San Francisco's Chinatown that the Chinese children there are similarly restrained and rarely fight over toys, and we have made similar observations in nursery schools in Hong Kong and Shanghai. Although there is substantial cultural continuity between the Chinese communities in Shanghai, Hong Kong, San Francisco, and Chicago, therefore, the fact that Chinese newborns already show a disposition toward relative nonexcitability and accomodation to external change leads logically to a genetic hypothesis with regard to these Chinese–Caucasian differences.

However, it must again be pointed out that any phenotype is subject to change, depending on the interaction of the genotype and environment ($P = G \times E$). A recent study conducted by Kuchner (1974) indicates that the presumed Chinese–Caucasian differences in temperament are no exception to this rule. In a study conducted in Chicago, Kuchner observed Chinese and Caucasian newborns in their families from birth through 5 months of age, focusing on mother–infant interactions. All families were upper middle class. In her initial report of this ongoing study, she stated that whereas many of the differences on the Cambridge Scales reported above were also exhibited by the newborns she studied, relatively few differences were to be seen in mother's attitudes toward the infants. All mothers, whether Chinese or Caucasian, had become "Americanized" and formed a more or less homogeneous group.

Nevertheless, Kuchner found that Chinese mothers interacted less with their infants than did the Caucasian mothers, even as Caudill and Weinstein (1969) had reported for a group of Japanese mothers in Japan who were compared with a group of American Caucasian mothers. Kuchner, however, suggests that the reason for this finding among her groups is that the Chinese infants were on the average, less evocative. In a preliminary analysis of five Chinese and five Caucasian babies matched for sex and birth order, Caucasian babies changed state more frequently, had longer average active periods, spent more of the diapering time active or fussy, and spent less time asleep or crying and more time in an awake, alert state. These differences follow rather directly on the differences found in temperament at birth, and they seem adequate to account for the differential interactions between mothers and infants. Although the process of "Americanization" may achieve a common endpoint in the child-rearing attitudes of mothers of different ethnic groups, child-rearing practices may nevertheless differ because of differences in the infants themselves.

This same reasoning probably accounts for the aforementioned study by Caudill and Weinstein (1969) on Japanese–Caucasian differences at 3 months of age, although the authors have thought differential maternal treatment to be the sole cause.

In general, there can be no doubt that heredity and culture interact as a feedback process, and that each contributes to the other in a multitude of ways. This chapter, then, is not intended as an argument for genetic determinism; instead, its intention is to call into question explanations based solely on cultural determinism.

What might be some cultural consequences of these average differences in temperament between Chinese and Caucasian newborns? Certainly we are here stepping into an arena already rife with speculation, but one's most immediate thoughts might center about Eastern versus Western art, even as it has occurred to Northrop (1960) in his *The Meeting of East and West.* In classic Chinese painting, the human figure, if it is central, is always formalized as if to deny its individuality. In landscape art, which is far more prevalent, humans are invariably represented by stick figures that blend into the majesty of the landscape. The ego of man is always subdued and hidden.

By contrast, the individualized hero is seen everywhere in Western art, ranging from the great Greek and Roman warrior sculptures through the awesome holy figures of Michaelangelo's Sistene Chapel. Even the frequent theme of the *Pièta* is a focus on the suffering of perhaps the greatest individualist of our time, the Christ. Contrast his active lifetime with

Buddha's achievements, which were entirely accomplishments of the contemplative mind.

As has been said by many, whereas Western man in his hubris has attempted to dominate nature, Eastern thought has emphasized the oneness of man and nature (cf. Nakamura, 1964; Chiang, 1960). For example, Western philosophy has consistently held to rational goals, culminating in modern science with its aim of explaining and controlling natural processes. By contrast, the Orient, until very recently, took a personal, esthetic view of nature (Northrop, 1960) and exhibited an antiscientific bias as far back as Lao-Tzu (400 B.C.):

> Whenever someone sets out to remold the world, experience teaches that he is bound to fail.
> For Nature already is as good as it can be.
> It cannot be improved upon.
> He who tries to redesign it, spoils it.
> He who tries to redirect it, misleads it. [Lao-Tzu, 1958, Verse 29]

Do we see the beginnings of these diverse forms of art and thought in newborn differences? We may never know for sure, but at least it makes sense that cultures invent philosophy and art in their own image, and that biology and culture tend to accomodate one to the other.

Incidentally, a group of Navajo newborns were much like the Chinese sample in that they, too, were relatively placid and accomodated readily to testing procedures to which Caucasian infants (as well as Nigerian and Australian aboriginal infants) severely "objected" (Freedman, 1974). The Navajo are an Athapaskan people, Asiatic in origin, and to this day we can discern some cognates between spoken Navajo and spoken Chinese. Certainly, the overall relatedness of Athapaskan languages and primitive Sino-Tibetan is clear (Shafer, 1952).

A followup study over the first year of life among 16 Navajo newborns, then, yielded some interesting reinterpretations with regard to cradleboarding and temperament. It has been noted frequently that very young Navajo children already exhibited traditional Indian stoicism and equanimity, and it is speculated that this may result from an infancy of confinement to the cradleboard. Our observations, however, indicate the obverse—that only those infants who do not complain are maintained in the cradleboard, and that Navajo mothers generally gauge release time by the complaints of the baby. Babies who never complain may be maintained on the cradleboard for as much as a year, whereas active complaining babies may be finished with the cradleboard by 3 months of age. The amount of time a baby is kept on the board per day is similarly determined largely by the baby himself. Although it is clear that bundling and cradleboarding tend to quieten babies (compare Lipton & Steinschneider,

1964), it appears nevertheless that cradleboarding is an institution maintained largely by the placid Navajo temperament, rather than vice versa.

In closing this section, we can only stress again that men everywhere are much more alike than they are different. Lewontin's (1971) analysis of 17 widely sampled blood factors (gene loci) showed that each major racial group within itself can account for 93.7% of all human genetic variation. There is, however, no point in ignoring the differences should one want to study them, provided that the questions asked are potentially constructive ones.

IS THERE A BIOLOGICAL BASIS FOR CULTURAL DIFFERENCES IN SEX ROLES?

We are concerned here, in a sense, with the opposite problem to that of the last section, that of invariance between cultures. Is there a commonality in sex-role differentiation around the world? According to a generation of opinion within cultural anthropology, the answer is no, for a dogma has developed over the past 20 years that sex role is highly malleable, if not specific to each culture.

Our own explanation of sex role starts with the recent work of Trivers (1972). He points out that throughout the animal kingdom, male and female roles differ depending on differential investment in care of offspring. If the male, for example, is the primary caretaker of the young, as in the phalarope, a shorebird, then the primary investment of the other sex, in this case the female, is in achieving a maximal number of matings. For example, in the phalarope, after she has laid her egg and is assured that the male is incubating, the female flies off in search of another mate and continues this behavior until the season's end.

As we all know, this case is an exception, for usually it is the male that expresses polygamous behavior, or at least polygamous intentions. Even in monogamous species of birds, there is still a greater tendency for the male to look for other amorous relations, particularly when the female is caring for the young. When the reproductive strategy of a species involves temporary liaisons, moreover, it is almost always the male who is more active sexually. The reason for this seems to be that the male's reproductive potential is vastly greater than the female's in all known species (some insects and single-celled creatures aside). In the human, the female's theoretical maximum is about 60 offspring, whereas a male, theoretically, could fecundate countless females. In a polygynous culture, he would be limited only by the number of his wives.

One of the consequences of such a strategy for survival is that males fall into competition with one another as each seeks to maximize offspring, whereas females can remain relatively noncompetitive because of their reproductive potential is near maximum anyway. There are many male–male aggressive displays, therefore, and in birds selection for greater male size, aggressivity, bright coloration, and song is at least as adaptive in warding off other males as it is in attracting females. Also, to the extent that the male of any species spends less time in parental care, he is expendable, and most species show greater male mortality (Trivers, 1972).

Among social animals, ranging from gallinaceous birds through the primates, male–male aggression has been modified into a dominance–submission hierarchy (known as a "pecking order" in chickens). The role of the females in these hierarchies varies with species, but she rarely participates with the same gusto as do the males and, as we shall see, this is true in man as well. Recent studies with baboons indicate that males at the top of the hierarchy do indeed fecundate females at a greater rate than do lower ranking members, so similar ends are achieved as in territorial, polygamous birds.

Let us now consider the human version of all this. It appears from the studies that we and others are doing that man is just another terrestrial primate when it comes to the development of dominance hierarchies. We have found that boys of 3 and 4 years are already vying with one another, and when two male 4-year-olds were asked "Which of you is toughest?" in 60% of the pairs, each answered "Me!" By 6 years of age, however, the same pairs of boys now tended to agree that one or the other was toughest, and a clear-cut hierarchy was seen in every classroom studied. A common figure was 80% agreement among the children in ranking the entire class on toughness (Omark & Edelman, 1973).

Interestingly, although for the most part girls ranked at the lower half of the hierarchy, their accuracy (agreement) in ranking was also about 80%. In general, all children showed greatest agreement about the higher ranking boys and the disagreements in ranking were largely over lower ranking individuals. In the words of Chance and Jolly (1970), there is an "attention structure" in primate hierarchies, with attention invariably focused on the most powerful; in this regard, man is like any other primate.

One other very human tendency emerges from these studies. The tendency for males, in particular, to rank themselves higher than others generally rank them. We call this phenomenon "overrating," and it is similar to the behavior of the 4-year-old boys, each of whom insists he is toughest. It appears that the majority of boys start with an inordinately high opinion of their own powers, and although this is subsequently modified by experience the tendency to overrate is probably never completely lost.

Girls, in contrast, were not as emotionally involved in ranking themselves. For example, although girls agreed that they would like to be known as "nicest," they never developed a competition about ranking themselves on this trait. Indeed, it would be ironical to see two contestants squabbling over which are "nicest."

It certainly appears that, at a very early age, boys and girls exhibit decidedly different social strategies, with boys more aggressively competitive and girls more oriented toward the social networks, the relationships and friendships that run their course over the school year (Stevens, 1972).

There are now socioeconomic class and cross-cultural data that corroborate these initial findings with children at the University of Chicago Laboratory Schools. The very same patterns have been found in lower class schools totally populated by Afro-American students, in white middle-class schools, and within grades and ungraded classes. Replication in a Zurich school and in an Ethiopian village school also yielded the same patterns (Omark, Omark, & Edelman, in press).

Furthermore, extensive notes on the play of 5- to 7-year-olds were made on playgrounds in Kyoto (Japanese), Delissaville (Australian Aborigine), Hong Kong (Chinese), Bali, Ceylon, New Delhi, Pondicherry, Kenya (Kikuyu), and Crown Point, New Mexico (Navajo). All yielded similar boy–girl differences in play patterns already familiar from our United States Caucasian and Afro-American observations. In each of these settings, boys were more aggressive with one another, ran in larger groups, and covered more physical space. Girls tended to hold more conversations with their nearest neighbor and engaged more in games or activities involving repeated movements or patterns, whereas boys tended to more physical interaction and less predictable activities. Some self-segregation of sexes was seen everywhere, less among the Kikuyu and greatest in Ceylon, but in all settings boys tended to play with boys and girls with girls. The cross-cultural continuities were, then, substantial.

Table 2.1 represents an analysis of free drawings ("Draw anything you want to draw") from each of these settings, and certain consistencies are clear. Boys everywhere drew more male figures, girls more female figures (as in Figures 2.1, 2.3, and 2.4). This may, of course, represent a projection of the self, and it may also be a reflection of the tendency for like-sexed children of this age to seek one another out.

Girls drew flowers more often. In Bali, Ceylon, and India, it should be noted, boys also consistently drew them (as in Figures 2.1, 2.2, 2.7, 2.8, 2.9, and 2.10), but unlike the girls, flower-drawing boys tended to include moving vehicles in their scenes as well (as in Figure 2.2). Where drawings tended towards "lists" of objects, as in Bali, boys would list a series of flowers, as did nearly all the girls, but interspersed among them (40% of the time) were vehicles (as in Figures 2.7 and 2.8). Even among the matriarchal Navajo, where about 30% of the girls drew vehicles, boys drew still more (54%). Additionally, Navajo boys also drew more horses.

TABLE 2.1
Sex Differences in Free Drawings over Nine Cultures; Comparative Percentages in the Five Most Consistently Differentiating Categories (12 categories were scored)

	Sex	American (Chicago) (ages 5–7)	Ceylonese (Kandy) (5–7)	Aborigine (Arnheim) (5–7)	African (Kikuyu) (5–7)	Indian (Delhi) (5–7)	Balinese (Batuan) (5–7)	Chinese (Hong Kong) (5–7)	American Indian (Navajo) (5–7)	Japanese (Kyoto) (3–6)
Vehicles	M	15.0%	68.4	48.6	86.4	33.8	41.6	17.0	54.0	33.3
	F	0.0[a]	7.1[a]	3.5[a]	61.9[a]	11.6[a]	1.0[a]	6.0[a]	29.0[a]	12.12
Monsters	M	15.0	0.0	5.4	0.0	5.6	10.5	10.6	2.0	57.1
	F	3.1	0.0	0.0	0.0	12.5	0.0	4.0	0.0	12.5[a]
Flowers	M	10.0	63.2	5.4	3.7	73.2	80.2	19.1	2.0	23.8
	F	21.9	78.6	31.0[a]	3.2	79.1	95.1[a]	54.0[a]	9.7	75.0[a]
Male figures	M	40.0	21.1	5.4	3.7	18.3	1.2	25.5	32.0	19.0
	F	3.12[a]	14.3	6.9	1.6	12.8	1.0	4.0[a]	22.6	0.0
Female figures	M	5.0	10.5	8.1	4.9	4.3	1.2	4.2	0.0	4.8
	F	65.6[a]	14.3	44.8[a]	3.2	33.7[a]	0.0	22.0[a]	9.7	93.8[a]
Number of subjects	M	20	19	37	81	71	86	47	50	21
	F	32	14	29	63	86	70	50	31	16

[a] $p < .05$.

FIGURE 2.1 Indian girl, Punjabi, New Delhi, 5½ years, colored crayons: "Teacher with a baby, sun, butterfly and flowers."

FIGURE 2.2 Indian boy, Punjabi, New Delhi, 6 years, colored crayons: "My house—my daddy is going in the plane to Calcutta."

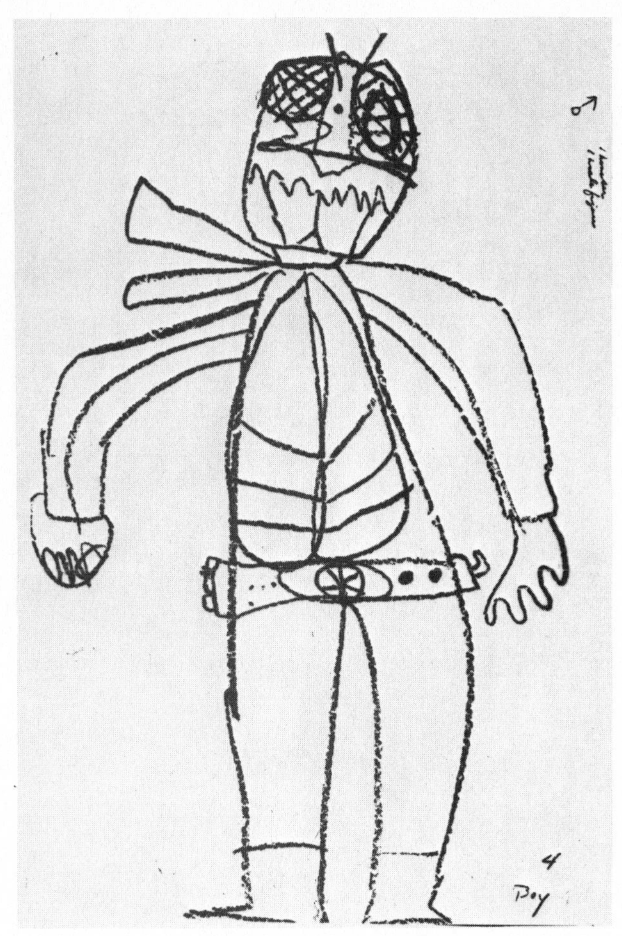

FIGURE 2.3 Japanese boy, Kyoto, 4 years, red crayon (a commonly drawn television monster hero).

In interpreting these data, it is important to note that among the Navajo, as many women as men actually drive vehicles, and both sexes learn to drive or ride horses at about the same age.

Our conclusions are similar to Erikson's (1975), and it seems a good possibility that these cross-culturally consistent sex differences reflect psychobiological differences. As is now well known, Erikson (1975) asked 11-, 12-, and 13-year-olds one at a time to arrange toys and blocks into "an exciting scene from an imaginary moving picture [p. 229]." Boys tended to build tall, often precarious towers and girls rather more peaceful, peopled enclosures, and Erikson related this to "unconscious," biological sex differences. Inasmuch as statements on sex differences are, at present, rapidly politicized, he has been somewhat villified for these conclusions

FIGURE 2.4 Japanese girl, Kyoto, 4 years, colored crayons.

FIGURE 2.5 African girl, Kikuyu, Kenya, 7 years, blue and yellow crayon (pathways joining houses are nearly always present in both sexes).

FIGURE 2.6 African boy, Kikuyu, Kenya 6 years, black and yellow crayon.

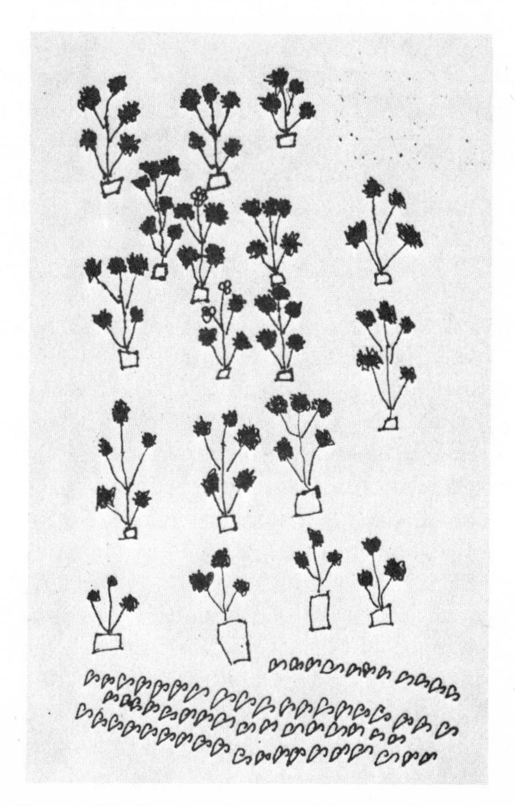

FIGURE 2.7 Balinese girl, Batuan, 7 years, blue magic marker (some 75% of Batuan drawings could not be distinguished from this one in either style or content).

FIGURE 2.8 Balinese boy, Batuan, 7 years, violet crayon.

(Erikson, 1975). Nevertheless, when Garai and Scheinfeld (1968) claim that males everywhere exhibit greater attraction to and interest in the display of aggression, and when Mead (1939) notes that it is the tendency for young males everywhere to travel further from the hearth, they may well be speaking of biologically based tendencies which also underlie these differences in drawings and play constructions.

In what might seem a contradiction, Kikuyu girls drew either as many or more vehicles than did the males of all but their own culture (as in Figures 2.5 and 2.6). They were, however, by far the most aggressive girls in the study, as judged by playground activity, and Kikuyu males reached the highest level of all in vehicular content. Aside from the obvious hypothesis that living in Tigoni, Kenya may be directly responsible for the interest in trucks, or that the vehicular motif is somehow institutionalized at the school, one can also hypothesize that the Kikuyu may be more androgenic as a group. The idea is at least open to research.

The cross-cultural strategy, then, is one approach to the question of built-in sex differences. Another is seeing whether sex differences appear

FIGURE 2.9 Chinese girl, Hong Kong, 6 years, pastel crayons (drawings in both sexes typically filled the entire space).

FIGURE 2.10 Chinese boy, Hong Kong, 7 years, pastel crayons.

early enough so that social learning is unlikely. Girls, in fact, are already more socially perceptive as infants, to judge by the work of Michael Lewis (1969). Lewis found that 6-month-old girls prefer to look at models of human faces, whereas 6-month-old boys look at inanimate objects or faces with equal interest. Lewis also reports (personal communication 1974) that if two adults hold a conversation before a 9-month-old female, she responds only when directly addressed. Nine-month-old boys, however, seem not to be able to discern as well when they are spoken to, and may "join in" at any time. Infant girls form words before boys, and it is by now well established that girls have a greater facility with language which continues throughout their lives (cf. Garai & Scheinfeld, 1968).

With regard to social adeptness, females have demonstrated a lower threshold to smiling in social encounters in five separate studies we have done. In one study (McLean, 1970), yearbook pictures at the University of Chicago High School and College were examined from 1931 through 1965, and in every series there were more smiling females than males. The differences were statistically significant in 13 of the 15 yearbooks examined. We have since examined yearbooks from lower class schools in Chicago and from an Australian aboriginal high school in Darwin and found the same pattern. In another study, the investigator simply clocked persons passing a busy intersection, and yet another involved counting returned smiles to the male and female experimenters. In both investigations, females exhibited significantly more smiling than did males.

Additionally, we have gathered evidence that, like the fear grin in monkeys, the smile is more readily exhibited by someone lower on the "toughness" hierarchy towards someone higher as a gesture of appeasement. When we paired children of the same sex or opposite sex and measured who stared at whom and who smiled at whom, Chance's hypothesis of "attention structure" was completely borne out. Those lower in the hierarchy looked at and smiled at those higher with far greater frequency than the reverse. Girls tended to be in the lower half and they smiled more in this study as well (Beekman, 1970).

These data, coupled with the astounding fact that even as newborns females show more reflexive smiling (Freedman, 1974), suggest that there must be some natural differences in how the average male and female enter a social encounter. If it is true that the function of smiling is to reduce aggression and assure the other of one's positive intentions, then females are greater specialists in getting along than are males.

A similar conclusion was reached by Parsons and Bales (1955), who felt that females everywhere took on a more expressive role and males a more instrumental role. Agreeing that the two attributes are always in combination within any individual, Parsons and Bales (1955) state:

> . . . the area of instrumental function concerns relations of the system to the situation outside the system, to meeting the adaptive conditions of its maintenance of equilibrium, and instrumentally establishing the desired relations to external goal objects. The expressive area concerns the "internal" affairs of the system, the maintenance of integrative relations between the members, and regulation of the patterns and tension levels of its component units [p. 47].

Within this instrumental–expressive dichotomy lies a great array of possibilities, in that the modal men and modal women of a society can conceivably vary from extreme male–instrumental and female–expressive to near equal combinations of each. However, the evidence is that reversals in these male and female modalities within a society is not probable.

Said another way, we are acknowledging here the importance of social learning and societal input in the patterning of variation in male and female roles, but we are at the same time emphasizing that societal institutions do not arise, as it were, out of the blue; and that world-wide consistencies in institutionalized male–female roles appear to reflect phylogenetically adaptive differences in the sexes, differences that may already be seen in their incipient forms in very early infancy.

REFERENCES

Beekman, S. The relation of gazing and smiling behavior to status and sex in interacting pairs of children. Unpublished master's thesis, Committee on Human Development, University of Chicago, 1970.

Brazelton, T. B., & Freedman, D. G. The Cambridge neonatal scales. In J. J. van der Werff ten Bosch (Ed.), *Normal and abnormal development of brain and behavior*. Leiden: Leiden University Press, 1971.

Caudill, W., & Weinstein, H. Maternal care and infant behavior in Japan and America. *Psychiatry,* 1969, **32,** 12–43.

Chance, M., & Jolly, C. J. *Societies of monkeys, apes and men*. New York: Dutton, 1970.

Chiang, I. *The Chinese eye; an interpretation of Chinese painting*. London: Methuen, 1960.

Chomsky, N. A. *Aspects of the theory of syntax*. Cambridge, Mass.: MIT Press, 1965.

Erikson, E. H. *Life History and the historical moment*. New York: Norton, 1975.

Freedman, D. G. *Human infancy: An evolutionary perspective*. Hillsdale, New Jersey: Lawrence Erlbaum Associates, 1974.

Fuller, J. L., & Thompson, W. R. *Behavior genetics*. New York: Wiley, 1960.

Garai, J. E., & Scheinfeld, A. Sex differences in mental and behavioral traits. *Genetics of Psychology Monographs,* 1968, **77,** 169–299.

Goldstein, K. *The organism*. Boston: Beacon Press, 1963.

Green, N. An exploratory study of aggression and spacing behavior in two preschool nurseries: Chinese-American and European-American. Unpublished master's thesis, Committee on Human Development, University of Chicago, 1969.

Hirsch, J. *Behavior-genetic analysis.* New York: McGraw-Hill, 1967.

Kuchner, J. Doctoral dissertation in progress. Department of Behavioral Sciences, University of Chicago, 1974.

Lao-Tzu. *Tao Teh King.* (Trans. by A. J. Bahm) New York: Frederick Ungar, 1958.

Lewis, M. Infants' responses to facial stimuli during the first year of life. *Developmental Psychology,* 1969, **2,** 75–86.

Lewontin, R. C. The apportionment of human diversity. *Evolutionary Biology,* 1971, **6,** 381–398.

Lipton, E. L., & Steinschneider, A. Studies in the psychophysiology of infancy. *Merrill-Palmer Quarterly,* 1964 **10,** 102–117.

McLean, J. D. Sex-correlated differences in human smiling behavior: A preliminary investigation. Unpublished manuscript, Committee on Human Development, University of Chicago, 1970.

McNeill, D. *The acquisition of language.* New York: Harper & Row, 1970.

Mead, M. *From the South Seas: Studies of adolescence and sex in primitive societies.* New York: W. Morrow, 1939.

Nakamura, H. *Ways of thinking of Eastern peoples: India, China, Tibet, Japan.* Honolulu: East–West Center Press, 1964.

Northrop, F. S. C. *The meeting of East and West: An inquiry concerning world understanding.* New York: Macmillan, 1960.

Omark, D. R., & Edelman, M. S. Peer group formation in young children; I. Action. II. Perception. Unpublished doctoral dissertations, Committee on Human Development, University of Chicago, 1973.

Omark, D. R., Omark, M., & Edelman, M. S. Formation of dominance hierarchies in young children: Action and perception. Paper presented at the IXth International Congress of Anthropological and Ethnological Sciences, Chicago, 1973. To be published in T. Williams (Ed.), *Psychological anthropology.* The Hague: Mouton Press, in press.

Parsons, T., & Bales, R. *Family socialization and interaction process.* Glencoe, Ill.: Free Press, 1955.

Shafer, R. Athapaskan and Sino-Tibetan. *International Journal of American Linguistics,* 1952, **18,** 12–19.

Stevens, C. An ethological investigation of social interaction among third graders. Unpublished master's thesis, Committee on Human Development, University of Chicago, 1972.

Trivers, R. L. Parental investment and sexual selection. In B. Campbell (Ed.), *Sexual selection and the descent of man, 1871–1971.* Chicago: Aldine, 1972. Pp. 136–179.

Comments on "Infancy, Biology, and Culture"

Joseph J. Campos

In the last few years, developmental psychologists have been utilizing the heuristic procedure of reconceptualizing the direction of causality in some important psychological propositions. Three recent examples immediately come to mind. In the field of parent–child relations, child psychologists had always assumed that a child's behavior was a function of that of his parents. However, in 1968, Bell presented evidence to indicate that at least some parental behaviors were directly instigated by the behavior of their children. In perceptual development, most of us had learned to accept the hypothesis that the sense of touch was developmentally primary and that we learned to see form and depth by association of vision with touch. Now Bower (1974) has begun to investigate how it may be vision that is developmentally primary, that is, how it is dominant over touch even in the very young infant. In the field of learning, ethologists have taken studies of conditioning of the smile in the infant and have concluded that the smile may not be so much a function of reinforcing social consequences as elicited by them.

Freedman seems to adopt a similar strategy to reconceptualize one aspect of the persistent nature–nurture controversy. He presents evidence that culture, an ultimate explanatory construct of the nurturists, may well be determined by the genetic traits that a newborn brings to the world, traits that result from selective inbreeding in racial subgroups, such as Chinese–American and European–American subjects. In the battle between the nativists and empiricists, this argument constitutes an attack behind the front lines of the empiricists, it seems to me.

Freedman's argument is ingenious and plausible. Nevertheless, some aspects of it require much supporting research before it can be given great confidence. The assumption that culture, language, and learning must all have a biological basis can be accepted readily, of course. All human activity must have a physiological correlate. However, the chapter subtly shifts the discussion from the biological bases of behavior to the genetic ones, and so it is likely to elicit more debate. For example, the study contrasting the behaviors of Chinese–American and European–American neonates may have found biologically based differences, but these differences may not necessarily be genetic in origin. Culture could be associated with different prenatal environments (e.g., because of different diets or emotions) that could create nongenetic but nevertheless biological differences in the offspring prior to birth. If this is so, the study of neonates may not be as free of social molding as may first appear. In other words, Freedman's study may have shown temperament to be innate but not that it necessarily is hereditary.

Freedman implicitly recognizes possibilities such as this one. Although he seems, overall, to be advocating a genetic basis for temperament, he does caution that his argument is not primarily intended to favor genetic determinism. His purpose, rather, is to show how differences in culture can ensue from differences in temperament. He also acknowledges that "heredity and culture interact as a feedback process," a proposition that, I think, has enormous implications for further freeing psychologists from the "either–or" mentality that has categorized many nature–nurture arguments of the past and present.

This implication should be spelled out, because with this statement Freedman goes not only beyond the time-worn thesis that culture influences behavior, but also beyond his own antithesis that heredity can influence culture. The synthesis suggested is that of a constant, spiraling process in which the biologically given traits interact with the cultural setting in a constant fashion throughout development (perhaps prenatally as well as postnatally, as alluded to earlier). Consider the study he cites on differences between the behaviors of Chinese–American and European–American parents toward their respective children. Chinese–American parents were found to interact less with their children than did European–Americans. This was said to result from the children of Chinese–Americans making fewer demands on their parents. If this is so, then the child's temperament is clearly determining his parents' behavior. However, because no one (and certainly not Freedman) has denied the importance of parental influences on behavior, this study ultimately suggests to the reader that the process of causation does not end with the children's temperament. Instead, the parents may continue to be important, if not for initiating their children's innate behavior at least for maintaining it.

If this is the case, then Freedman's implicit position in this paper may be very similar to that espoused recently by Sameroff and Chandler

(1975). According to these authors, prenatal and perinatal biological casualties have rarely been found to have great predictive impact in the absence of understanding of the social and emotional environment in which a child with such a casualty is reared. They were persuaded that mechanistic, unidirectional views of cause and effect explain little in studies of high-risk infants. When they tried to see whether characteristics of infants were predictive of later developmental abnormalities, they were disappointed to find few positive findings. When they looked for characteristics of the caretaking environment by itself, they again found few relationships with later developmental abnormalities in children. Only when they considered (a) the characteristics of both the individual and the caretaking environment and (b) the continuous, circular process of the child constantly affecting the environment and the environment constantly affecting the child did they find successful predictions of later developmental abnormality. Sameroff and Chandler consequently adopted what they called a transactional model, heavily influenced by Waddington's (1957) conception of the role of gene action in development.

In his chapter, Freedman has succeeded in reversing the usual thinking that psychologists have had about the role of culture and has explicitly (although briefly) acknowledged the interactive feedback between heredity and culture. As a result, we may be one step closer to a more dynamic conception of genetic–environment interaction, such as has been posited by Waddington, Sameroff, and Chandler, and now by Scarr-Salapatek in her contribution to this volume.

REFERENCES

Bell, R. Q. A reinterpretation of the direction of effects in studies of socialization. *Psychological Review,* 1968, **75,** 81–95.

Bower, T. G. R. *Development in infancy.* San Francisco: W. H. Freeman, 1974.

Sameroff, A. J., & Chandler, M. J. Perinatal risk and the continuum of caretaking casualty. In F. Horowitz, M. Hetherington, S. Scarr-Salapatek, & G. Siegel (Eds.), *Review of child development research.* Vol. 4. Chicago: University of Chicago Press, 1975. Pp. 187–244.

Waddington, C. H. *The strategy of the genes.* New York: Macmillan, 1957.

3

Genetic Determinants of Infant Development: An Overstated Case

Sandra Scarr-Salapatek

University of Minnesota

Psychology seems to be in the midst of an aperiodic swing between extreme forms of environmentalism and hereditarianism. More biological assumptions, variables, methods, and conclusions have crept into child development during the past 10 years than in the preceding 25. Although a welcome corrective, this trend toward psychobiology should be critically evaluated. We must first be alert to the dangers of reductionism inherent in biological explanations of behavioral phenomena. Second, we must avoid an extreme form of genetic determinism that ignores the necessary transactions between genotypes and their environments throughout the lifespan of development and ignores the important variations that exist among individuals. A serious appraisal of contemporary biology and genetics avoids both of these errors.

Explanations of behavioral phenomena may include variables derived from other levels of analysis, but their effects must be explained at a behavioral level. Genetic effects on behavior are plausible only as the explanation incorporates biochemical pathways to morphological characteristics (e.g., brain structures) that mediate the gene–behavior links. Even if current knowledge precludes a complete explanation, the partial understanding must incorporate hypothetical links from gene constituents to the behavioral level of organization. Genes do not act directly on behavior, and theoretical statements should not be reductionist in this sense.

Another source of confusion in earlier hereditarian eras arose from the failure to understand Darwinian theory. The two indispensible principles of evolution are *variation* and *selection*. The older, Platonic stance of the physical sciences, which was emulated by the behavioral sciences, held that variations are merely imperfect reproductions of the ideal type (shadows on the cave wall). Darwin's great insight was that the "ideal" was merely an abstraction from the fact of individual variation. Without genetic variation, selection through differential fertility could not operate and evolution could not occur. All natural populations contain enormous genetic variability.

Early hereditarians neglected the importance of variation and described "instinctive" behaviors as though each species had an ideal type that individuals only approximate. Typological thinking still persists in psychology, as in references to the 3-month-old, generalized laws of learning across species, and categorical sex differences. Darwin's insight led to population concepts, statistical statements about the distribution of individual differences in a population. Whereas distributions have central tendencies, they also have variances. The latter supply more information about the origins of the behaviors. Through studies of related and unrelated persons in same and different environments, proportions of variance can be assigned to genetic and environmental causes. Although specific gene loci are seldom identified for behavioral variation in the normal range, at least the biometrical approach can answer some questions about the general sources of existing variation.

Tracing causal pathways from gene to behavioral levels has not been notably successful for the many gene loci that affect normal behaviors, despite the considerable success of the Mendelian approach in the study of single aberrant genes associated with deviant phenotypes. There are, of course, variations among the phenotypes associated with a single aberrant gene, which suggests that other genes and environmental factors contribute to the phenotypic development of even deviant life forms. Whether a Mendelian approach to normal behavior can be fruitful remains to be seen.

Given the continued conflict between typological (Platonic) and population (Aristotelian) concepts (e.g., Revusky, 1974), it is not surprising that causal explanations of the "typical" development of human infants often fall into a philosophical trap. First, although we like to talk about causes of development, our scientific methods are best suited to the study of differences, not development. Second, accounting for variability is logically prior to an adequate explanation of development, which must encompass the sources of variation before abstracting a "typical" pattern of developmental causes. However, identifying sources of variation does not explain development. Behavioral scientists are therefore prone to commit two kinds of errors: to jump from central tendencies to determinants of development with nary a thought for variation, and to jump from causes of variation to causes of development.

Understanding sources of variation within a population or between populations is difficult enough, but accounting for human development per se is a far more difficult task. Our scientific methods of analysis and synthesis are suited for the study of variation, not the causes of development. Causal research in psychology and genetics can be understood only in the context of differences. Intervention and field studies of the correlates of planned and observed environmental variation and genetic studies of the correlates of genotypic variation are obvious examples. Even experimental studies of developmental characteristics most often depend on differences among age groups, sexes, or some arbitrary "populations" to be more than descriptive accounts. (In most cases experimental studies illustrate typological thinking.)

Studies of variation, however well conceived and conducted, do not lead directly to an understanding of development per se. Sources of variation are unlikely to be a complete set of determinants for development at any level. One seldom includes cellular metabolism in a study of object concept development, yet it is very important to brain functioning and therefore intelligent behavior. Furthermore, other critical determinants of development may not vary in a population—many genes and environmental features that are critical to survival are shared by all members of the population. They will not be identified by studies of individual variation.

To identify the elements of developmental systems that are common to all members of the species is to define the species. Mayr (1970) has argued that species are best defined not by reproductive isolation from other species but by a shared developmental pattern. The shared developmental pattern for infant behavior can be described but not explained. An explanation, I argue, depends on our understanding of the elements of that developmental system, how they are organized, and how they change over time. We have not come close to such an understanding. To claim empirical support for genetic blueprints of development or for environmental determinants of development is to skip several essential steps in building an adequate theory of development.

Three important statements follow from the foregoing discussion:

1. We cannot hope to understand development unless we account for variation in development because there is no ideal type to discover.
2. Understanding variation is necessary but not sufficient for understanding development.
3. Understanding development necessitates models of complex sets of determinants at many levels, organized at a behavioral level, and governed by laws that change over time.

In this chapter, I hope to illustrate some problems in current empirical efforts to identify genetic determinants of development and to propose some partial solutions to conceptual problems in understanding variation and development.

SYSTEMS IN DEVELOPMENT

As Paul Weiss (1968) has argued so compellingly, living systems require explanations that account for their organization and their development. Simple, linear, cause–effect statements cannot fully explain the phenomena of growth at cellular, morphological, or behavioral levels. The mechanistic, deterministic view accounts for partial relationships among constituent parts of a system and between individual parts and the whole, but it cannot account for the organized course of development. The laws of organization at behavioral levels have not, to my knowledge, been adequately described. Although this deficit does not prevent us from believing intuitively that they are discoverable, it does impede research. Analysis and synthesis have served biologists and psychologists well and must continue to do so until scientific methods are adapted to systems theory. We can at least clear up our thinking on development, however, and restrict our empirical claims to statements that fit our current scientific methods.

No matter what the level of analysis, genes and environments are both required for development to occur and for life to be sustained. As Hebb (1970) has said, it is best to think of the determination of behavior as both 100% genetic and 100% environmental! Statements about genetic determinants, rather than differences, lead necessarily to a concern with genes as constituents in systems that always include environmental components as well. The evolving ontogenetic pattern that can be described by this approach is most often species typical.

There are a few beautiful examples of ethological studies that detail genetic mechanisms and environmental contexts for the evolution and development of animal behavior. Rothenbuhler (1967) described the fixed action patterns of hygienic honeybees who uncap and remove the dead larvae from cells in the comb. Through breeding experiments, he was able to identify two gene loci implicated in the two separable acts, uncapping and cleaning. In his work with parrots, Dilger (1962) discovered two alleles associated with nest building techniques. The alleles were identified by crossing two races of finches with different techniques. The resultant hybrids are best described as confused nest builders, uncertain about where and how to transport the required nesting materials. Chromosome mapping of behavioral traits in *Drosophila* strains is advanced (e.g., Benzer, 1973), but the difficulties inherent in studying the components of behavioral development, even in infrahuman species, are monumental.

The use of analytic strategies to study components of behavioral development raises extremely difficult problems of external validity, which virtually rules out the use of artificially inbred strains and uniform rearing conditions, and internal validity, which demands that both genetic and environmental parameters be systematically controlled. Deprivation experiments can demonstrate the disastrous effects of rearing conditions that deviate significantly from what is normal for the species, but they do not illuminate the effects of variation within the average range of environments. Field studies can demonstrate adaptational variation, but they do not separate the effects of genetic heterogeneity from environmental diversity.

Most ethologists have chosen to ignore the study of gene action, leaving that task to geneticists. Unfortunately, most geneticists are not equipped to study behavior, choosing instead simpler phenotypes for analysis. Developmental psychobiology has the opportunity to integrate the models and research methods from these several fields.

Some psychologists have studied the development of species-typical behavior, even if they have not claimed as much. Piaget's descriptions of intellectual development are ethological accounts of the human pattern. His is a systems approach (Piaget & Inhelder, 1969), but he has not yet detailed the constituents he believes to be involved in cognitive development. Modern linguistic theory is also a systems approach, including as one element the genetic predisposition of human infants to acquire a language. No one has yet specified, however, what genetic mechanisms must be involved in the readiness of all human infants to speak. Werner's organismic theory (Werner, 1961) is essentially a description of developing behavioral systems that subsume both genetic and experiential components. Again, the components are not described.

Biologically aware psychologists have noticed genetic constituents in the development of human behavior, but they have not generally dwelt on the role of genetic constituents as separable components in behavioral systems, nor have they dealt primarily with individual variation. In fact, it is probably unwise to emphasize either genetic or environmental components in the description of behavioral systems. Unless one can specify gene action pathways and critical environmental features, or at least apportion genetic and environmental variations, one is simply left with Hebb's tautology that, of course, behavioral development depends on both. If one is to use the study of differences to illuminate behavioral development, then the concepts and methods must be integrated and the inferences appropriately made.

OF CREODS AND COMMON HUMAN ENVIRONMENTS

Genes and Canalization

Human behavioral development is not a random set of changes but a highly organized pattern of steps and stages. To what extent has evolution limited the possible developmental responses of human organisms to their environments? By what mechanisms is the possible number of phenotypes less than infinite? These questions bring into focus several important concepts in development: canalization, reaction range, buffering, and expression.

Canalization is the genetic limitation of phenotypic development to a few possible phenotypes rather than an infinite variety. If genotypes had unlimited modifiability in response to environmental differences, phenotypic variability among species members would be vastly greater than it is. In fact, there is a limited repertory of human behaviors that we all recognize as "human" and that develops in all nondefective species members. The genetic restriction of possible phenotypes is a result of coadapted gene complexes (sets of genes that have evolved together) that buffer the developmental pattern against deviation outside of the normal, species range of variation. (Selection, of course, operates to eliminate genes associated with abnormal variants.) Considerable genetic variation can be maintained within the species as long as developmental pathways are canalized and phenotypes restricted to an adaptive range. Canalization also means that many genotypes are functionally equivalent in producing any given phenotype (Mayr, 1970).

Waddington (1971) has observed that canalization is one of the most obtrusive phenomena of development: ". . . The fact that there are alternative developmental pathways, rather than an infinite gamut of possibilities, is an inherent property of developing biological systems . . . [p. 20]."

The limitation of possible phenotypes to a few rather than many is a fact of genotypes' ranges of reaction. This concept can best be expressed developmentally in the notion of developmental pathways, which Waddington calls "creods." Behavioral creods are essentially similar to Piaget's notion of schemes, organized patterns of behavior that develop in characteristic ways. They represent the biases the organism has toward acquiring some rather than other forms of behavior.

These biases are undoubtedly genotypic. Waddington continued his description of creods by saying that:

> The degree to which each pathway is canalized or self-establishing is dependent on the particular alleles of the genes involved in it, and it can be altered by selection of a population either for alleles which fit better into

> the canalized system (and thus increase the organism's resistance of modification) or for alleles which do not integrate so well with the others (and thus lend to decreased resistance to external influences) [p. 20].

The major questions of this paper concern (1) the degree to which infant behavioral development can be said to be genotypically canalized; (2) the kind of evidence available to support a strong canalization position; and (3) the kind of evidence needed to evaluate the degree of canalization. Are genes the major constituents in developmental patterns and in the rates of development; that is, do genes control more of the variance than other elements in the development of infant behavioral systems?

The Evolutionary Context

Two facts of human evolutionary history are particularly salient for infancy: the necessity of infant–mother dyads and the consistent availability of a larger human group into which the dyad is integrated. No surviving infant was without a social context throughout human history. The evolution of infant development has occurred, therefore, in the context of normal infant environments. This context has, I think, profound implications for the lack of developmental fixity (Lehrman, 1970) in infant behavior. Foremost, it has been unnecessary for selection to build into the genotype those behaviors that all infants are going to develop experientially in their human groups. All normal infants would have close contact with mothers and other conspecifics, with tools, and with material culture, thus giving them opportunities to learn object manipulation, social bonds, and a human language. What has evolved genotypically is a bias toward acquiring these forms of behavior, which Dobzhansky (1967) calls human educability.

We seldom emphasize the role of common human environments in development, being attuned as we are to look at distinctive features. The environments for such highly canalized behaviors as walking are seldom even studied. Lipsitt (1971, p. 499) gave a charming description of an infant who is "ready" to walk being propped up on his legs and flopped back and forth between adults. The acquisition of walking undoubtedly has experiential components that can be studied (Zelazo, this volume). However, all human environments seem to provide the necessary and sufficient conditions for walking to begin between 10 and 15 months. Only physically infirm infants (handicapped, malnourished) and those deprived of firm support (Dennis, 1960) fail to walk during infancy.

A similar point can be made about language acquisition. All normal hearing infants have a human language environment, regardless of which language is spoken, that provides the necessary and sufficient conditions for acquisition. Infant intellectual development has some of the same properties in that it follows a species pattern of sensorimotor skills that assimilate whatever material objects the culture offers. The overall species patterns for motor, language, and cognitive development seem to be well ordered by the chromosomes and the common human environment. Although experimental interventions may accelerate the acquisition of these behaviors, all normal infants acquire them in due time, and it is not clear that acceleration has any lasting impact on subsequent development.

The species pattern does not preclude group differences in infant development, however, nor individual variation in development. Variation is a fact of nature, as Dobzhansky has said, and not a priori evidence for environmental differences (Dobzhansky, 1973). The importance of genetic variation, both between and within groups, is as serious a hypothesis as environmental or cultural differences.

The Functional Equivalence of Environments

Environments that have distinctive, describable differences may or may not be effectively different. The functional difference between environments is defined by their effects on development. Strong canalization implies that many environments are functionally equivalent—have equivalent effects on development.

An argument can be made in favor of the functional equivalence of many seemingly different environments for the development of walking, for example. The mere opportunity for bipedal locomotion may be sufficient. If parents actively participate in teaching the skill, there is question as to how much acceleration can be expected. Early language skills may have only the necessity of responsive adult verbalization to the infant, contingent on the infant's productions. Hearing infants of deaf parents seem to acquire normal language skills with only a few hours of verbal interaction per week (Lenneberg, 1967; Moores, personal communication, 1973). Viewed from a species level, infant cognitive skills develop in all human contexts.

The Functional Equivalence of Genotypes

Just as many differences observed among environments may not much affect individual infants' development, so may many different genotypes produce similar phenotypes. Depending on the definition of the phenotype, most or even all of the normal genotypes in a population may produce equivalent phenotypes (such as right handedness or walking in infancy).

For some features of behavior that are crucial to reproduction, there is little genetic variation in the species. For most behaviors, however, genetic variability is a fact of nature, even if it is not expressed in the range of environments provided. Much of our genetic variability is probably hidden by development in a limited range of environments (Thiessen, 1972).

How much of the existing variation one sees, and where, depends on how closely one looks. From a lofty ethological vantage point, comparisons among species can make individual variation within the species virtually invisible. For some phenotypes, both genotypes and environments can be functionally equivalent for the entire species. From a lower elevation human phenotypes appear more varied; subgroups may have distinctive average tendencies, and individuals form a kaleidoscopic array of variations on the species theme.

For example, the infant acquisitions of object concept and two-word sentences can be said to be highly canalized in that both have regular patterns of development for all normal members of the species; if one looks more closely, however, there are individual differences in rates of acquisition, and there may be group differences as well. Although both genotypes and environments may be equivalent for the overall species pattern, one or both may not be equivalent for the development of individual variants.

To make sense of studies that use the concept of canalization, one must pay careful attention to the level at which the concept is applied and to the way in which the phenotype is defined.

Canalization and Variation

Four operational definitions are proposed to integrate theoretical statements about canalization with studies of variation, including population and individual levels of analysis. First, functional equivalencies in both genotypes and environments are interpreted as strong canalization at the species level with little individual variation and low heritability. Second, functional differences in genotypes and equivalencies in environments are interpreted as strong canalization at the individual level. Characteristics with this pattern show high heritability within a population and between populations if the distribution of genotypes is different. Third, functional equivalencies in genotypes and differences in environments are interpreted as weak individual canalization, yielding low heritabilities. Fourth, functional equivalence of neither genotypes nor environments yields extreme variation at the individual phenotypic level, with the variation a result of both genotypes and environments.

The strong canalization hypothesis, therefore, can apply to the species, to breeding populations, and to individual levels of analysis. Studies of variation within given populations have usually attended to the individual level; cross-cultural studies have usually attended to the population level, and ethological studies to the species level. In the remainder of this chapter, I evaluate evidence that has been used to support a strong canalization position, particularly for infant mental development.

CANALIZATION OF INFANT MENTAL DEVELOPMENT

Wilson (1972a, b) has argued, on the basis of his data on twins' development, that infant mental development is highly canalized at the individual level, difficult to deflect from its genotypic course, and unaffected by differences in an average range of home environments:

> Therefore, the hypothesis is proposed that these socioeconomic and maternal care variables serve to modulate the primary determinant of developmental capability, namely, the genetic blueprint supplied by the parents. On this view, the differences between twin pairs and the similarities within twin pairs in the course of infant mental development are primarily a function of the shared genetic blueprint.
>
> Further, while there is a continuing interaction between the genetically determined gradient of development and the life circumstances under which each pair of twins is born and raised, it requires unusual conditions to impose a major deflection upon the gradient of infant development [Wilson, 1972a, p. 917].

The primacy of "genetic blueprints" for development is a view shared by Sperry (1971). With respect to the importance of infancy and early childhood, Sperry said:

> The commonly drawn inference in this connection is that the experiences to which an infant is subjected during these years are primary. I would like again to suggest that there might be another interpretation here, namely, that it is the developmental and maturational processes primarily that make these years so determinative.
>
> During the first few years, the maturational program is unraveling at great speed. A lot of this determination seems to be inbuilt in nature; this is becoming increasingly clear from infant studies. I think we ought to keep our minds open to the possibility that the impression these first years are so critical is based to a considerable extent on the rapid unraveling of the individual's innate character [p. 527].

Three lines of evidence that have been used to support a strong canalization position on infant mental development are family correlations, studies of individual consistency over time, and cross-cultural studies.

Family Studies

Table 3.1 shows the results of four family studies of twins and siblings, using infant mental tests.

TABLE 3.1
Infant Mental Scale Correlations for Related Pairs in the First Year of Life

Test	Age (months)	Twins			Siblings		Estimates of genetic variance		Reference
		MZ (N)	SSDZ (N)	OSDZ (N)	SS (N)	OS (N)	Twins 2(riMZ – riDZ)	Siblings 2(ri)	
Bayley	3	.84	.67				.34		Wilson (1972b)
	6	.82	.74				.16		
	9	.81 (~82)	.69 (~101)[a]				.24		
	12	.82	.61				.42		
Bayley									
Whites	8	.83 (48)	.51 (41)	.56 (62)	.17 (887)	.22 (939)	.64	.39	Broman *et al.* (1975)
Blacks	8	.85 (74)	.43 (47)	.57 (78)	.22 (656)	.16 (745)	.84	.38	
Total	8	.84 (122)	.46 (88)	.58 (140)	.21 (1543)	.20 (1684)	.76	.41	
Gesell	6 & 12				.24 (142)			.48	McCall (1972a)
Bayley	2–12	Variance within MZ pairs significantly lower than variance within DZ pairs (N = 20)							Freedman and Keller (1963)

[a] There were a few opposite-sex pairs included.

Wilson's conclusion about the "genetic blueprint" for development is based primarily on the very high monozygotic (MZ) correlations obtained on the same day by cotwins (Wilson & Harpring, 1972). The cotwin correlations at the same point in time were much higher, in fact, than the month-to-month correlations for the same infant.

Broman, Nichols & Kennedy, 1975 data from the collaborative study support Wilson's findings of high MZ correlations. Monozygotic twins could hardly be more similar. The two studies differ, however, in their results for dizygotic (DZ) pairs. The genetic correlation between DZ cotwins is estimated to be between .50 and .55, the larger figure based on parental assortative mating. However, note that Wilson's DZ pairs are considerably more similar than expected. Wachs (1972) replied that "This degree of correlation indicates the operation of nongenetic factors in the dizygotic twins' mental test performance." (p. 1005) Indeed, Nichols and Broman's dizygotic twins displayed the level of similarity predicted by a genetic model. Both same- and opposite-sexed twins have correlations of .50 ± .09, which are well within the 95% confidence interval around .5 in this study.

Now look at the siblings. Although they share the same percentage of genes in common, on the average, as dizygotic twins, the Fels and collaborative studies found them to be far less similar in mental development during infancy. When McCall (1972b) challenged Wilson's genetic interpretation of his twin results, Wilson (1972b) replied:

> The correlations reported by McCall for the Fels sibling pairs are so low, however, as to raise questions about the reliability of the scores, particularly if the tests were administered by different examiners over a long period. The Gesell does not lend itself to formal scoring as readily as the Bayley, and the reliability of the scoring method itself has been questioned [p. 1006].

There are three points to be made about the sibling versus DZ twin results. First, the Fels results from the Gesell tests are in good agreement with the definitive data from the collaborative study. With sample sizes between 656 and 939 pairs, Nichols and Broman reported average correlations of about .20 for siblings; McCall reported .24. There is no question that siblings are less similar than DZ twins and that the explanation must be based on the greater environmental similarity of twins, both pre- and postnatally. Second, the results of the Gesell examinations cannot be dismissed as unreliable if the Bayley results are essentially similar.

Third, and most provocative, is Wilson's suggestion that different examiners may have influenced the magnitude of differences between the Fels siblings. The collaborative study twins and siblings were also generally tested by different examiners (Broman *et al.*, 1975), and the siblings' differences were notably larger than those between DZ twins.

We are still left with very puzzling results. The maximum heritability that can be obtained for any characteristic is twice the sibling correlation (Falconer, 1960). This calculation assumes that all of the variance between siblings is genetic and that no environmental variance is present. For behavioral traits this is an absurd assumption, and the heritability should most often be less than twice the sibling correlation. A comparison of the McCall and Nichols and Broman sibling data with the latter's twin results will quickly show a substantial difference in calculated heritability. Twice the sibling correlation varies around .40; heritabilities based on the twin results are much higher, around .75.

Because twins are nearly always tested on the same day whereas siblings may be tested at slightly different ages, Broman *et al.* (1975) examined their data for age differences between siblings at testing, which were inconsequential. Then they tested for uniform correlations across the range of scores to assess the influence of extremely low scores. Extreme scores, which are much more frequent for twins in general, have also shown greater concordance than higher scores among MZ twins. After they had eliminated the twin pairs in which one or both scored less than 50, they found that the MZ correlation was reduced to .63 whereas the DZ correlation increased slightly to .57. Low scores had inflated the heritability estimate by a factor of six. Although the best estimate of heritability for a population should include some low scores, the distribution of scores in a twin sample should represent the population distribution. Broman *et al.* (1975) concluded: "These results suggest that the influence of genetics (differences) on scores on the Bayley Mental exam is greatest at the low end of the distribution, and underline the need for caution when interpreting twin correlations [p. 5]."

The hypothesis that a "genetic blueprint" programs infant mental development does not stand up as well as the high MZ correlations lead us to believe.

Canalization of patterns of infant mental development. There is an additional hypothesis that deserves mention: that patterns of change in infant mental development are programmed by the individual genotype. Waddington (1971) has proposed that the degree of canalization can vary depending on the alleles present at relevant loci, which suggests that some genotypes are better buffered than others. Wilson (1972a) found that the profiles of scores obtained from the MZ twins over the first 2 years were significantly more similar than those obtained from DZ pairs; that is, that MZ cotwins show more similar responses to their common environments. McCall (1970) found no similarity in sibling profiles of intellectual development. Apart from the methodological arguments, which I do not detail here (see McCall, 1970, 1972b; McCall, Appelbaum & Hogarty, 1973; Wilson, 1972b; Wilson & Harpring, 1972), there is a substantive question again about the interpretation of twin data. Cotwins must share very common rearing environments as well as genotypes. In infancy, the effects of shared prenatal environments may be more important than they are at later ages. Sibling data provide a crucial check on the generalization of twin results.

Every genotype, it is said, has its own range of reaction (Gottesman, 1963; Ginsburg, 1967). The lack of sibling similarity in patterns of development suggests that every genotype also has its unique developmental pathways in the absence of extremely similar environments. Common environments, however, such as those of twins, may "canalize" development nearly as much as common genotypes. How else are we to explain Wilson's DZ twins' profile correlations of .5 for the first and second years and McCall's sibling profile correlations that do not differ from zero? It seems likely that genetically induced profile similarity is unique to identical genotypes and that twin environments, both pre- and postnatal, can produce a phenocopy of canalization by limiting the environmental variation to which the different genotypes respond.

Continuity in Development

Continuity in developmental levels and profiles has been used as evidence for canalization. In longitudinal studies of singletons, less continuity of intellectual level has been found in infancy than in later years (Bayley, 1965). Although one recent study with a small sample failed to find any continuity (Lewis & McGurk, 1972), there are most often correlations of .2 to .6 in mental levels across the first 2 years. Wilson (1972a; Wilson & Harpring, 1972) has attributed the lower correlations between ages under 2 years to the genetic blueprint, which has genotypically different spurts and lags in its course. Others have argued for discontinuities in the skills being tested at various ages (Stott & Ball, 1965; McCall, Appelbaum, & Hogarty, 1973).

Sameroff and Chandler (1975) have presented a transactional model that ascribes consistency to both organismic variables and to caretaking environments that support and maintain responses in the system. For example, infants with "difficult" temperaments are more likely to evoke assaultative behavior from their caretakers, whose battering increases the probability of more maladaptive behavior by the infants, and so forth.

Continuity from infant to later development can be observed for some infants who score poorly on infant mental scales. They more often remain retarded than others who are not impaired in early life. However, the prediction from the first to later childhood is greatly enhanced by consideration of the caretaking environment, which if poor increases the risks for poor development of "retarded" infants (Sameroff & Chandler, 1975;

Scarr-Salapatek, 1973; Willerman, Broman, & Fiedler, 1970). Infants who perform poorly in the first year but who have middle-class families are rarely retarded by school age. Infants at risk for retardation whose families are lower class show greater continuity in poor development (Scarr-Salapatek, 1973; Willerman *et al.*, 1970). The reasons for later retardation may vary between middle-class and lower class groups, but the continuous caretaking environment is at least one apparent difference. It is not clear that continuity in infant mental development can be attributed primarily to genetic blueprints.

Cross-Cultural Studies

If infant development is highly canalized at a species level, one might expect to find universal patterns and rates of infant behavioral development, regardless of differences in child-rearing practices. No one has recently argued that the sequences of infant behavioral acquisitions are different across cultures. Piaget's (1952) descriptions of the important sensorimotor stages seem to apply to all normal infants. Differences in rates of development, however, have been noted for infants and older children of various cultural groups.

There are at least three problems with the cross-cultural paradigm in studies of canalization. First, genetic differences in rates of development may exist between populations. Relatively isolated gene pools may have evolved somewhat different patterns of infant development. Second, cross-cultural studies are fraught with methodological problems (Pick, in press; Warren, 1972) that may apply less to infant studies than to studies of older children but that cannot be ruled out entirely. Third, the cultural practices that may, in fact, affect rates of infant development may not be identified by investigators, who may be at a loss to know what comparisons to make. These three problems—possible genetic differences, methodological problems, and identification of relevant environmental contingencies—make the interpretation of cross-cultural research on infant development difficult.

Nevertheless, what has been observed? Kagan and Klein (1973) have published a cross-sectional study of infant and childhood intellectual development in Guatemala. Their assessment of infant development in an Indian village suggested to them that the children were behaviorally quite "retarded" at the end of the first year. Older children in the same setting, however, approached the performance levels of United States children on a variety of learning and perceptual tasks. From the observation of "retarded" infants and intellectually "normal" older children, they concluded that human development is inherently resilient; that is, highly canalized at the species level:

> This corpus of data implies that absolute retardation in the time of emergence of universal cognitive competences during infancy is not predictive of comparable deficits for memory, perceptual analysis, and inference during preadolescence. Although the rural Guatemalan infants were retarded with respect to activation of hypotheses, alertness, and onset of stranger anxiety and object permanence, the preadolescents' performance were comparable to American middle class norms. Infant retardation seems to be partially reversible and cognitive development during the early years more resilient than had been supposed [p. 957].

Kagan and Klein attribute the slow rate of behavioral development among rural Guatemalan infants to their being kept in darkened huts until the second year of life.

One can immediately see that longitudinal research may provide a stronger basis for inferences about the predictive significance of infant retardation. Where small samples are involved, sampling bias is a significant problem. A more crucial question can be raised about the adequacy of later assessments on which the authors have based their assertions that Guatemalan children score as well as whites from the United States. They acknowledge ceiling effects on their measures; in fact, it is not clear that Guatemalan children have in any sense a set of intellectual skills comparable to white children from the United States. When measures set the criterion of performance so low that nearly all children in both groups reach the ceiling on the tests, there is simply no way to assert that their performance levels are the same or different. Presumably, all normal 11-year-olds in the world have rudimentary number skills, but some may well understand complex formal operations and others have only the more elementary concepts of identity and associativity. If they are tested only on the elementary concepts, we cannot know whether they have the same level of mathematical skill or not.

What Kagan and Klein (1973) suggested about canalization is that the caretaking practices of rural Guatemalans significantly retard the rate of infant development, but that this deflection is only temporary because later child-rearing practices compensate for the early deprivation. In Waddington's terms, then, the Guatemalan infants' mental development is asserted to have been temporarily deflected from its canalized course by environmental deprivations but to have exhibited the same kind of "catch-up" phenomenon claimed for physical growth among children who have been ill or malnourished for brief periods of time. Unfortunately, we do not know if the older Guatemalan children have intellectual skills typical of white children from the United States, so that arguments for canalization seem inappropriate.

Is there good evidence from other studies for the strong canalization of any aspect of infant development at a population level? Can we distinguish cultural practices that accelerate or retard development from possible genetic differences in rates of growth?

Motor precocity. Infants in other groups have been observed to be accelerated or retarded in sensorimotor development, compared with white infants from the United States. African infants have often been found to be precocious (see Warren, 1972; Freedman, 1975), particularly in the early appearance of major motor milestones, such as sitting, standing alone, and walking. Although some investigators have related the precocity of African infants to child-rearing practices (Geber, 1958), black infants from the United States have also been found to be precocious in the same ways (Bayley, 1965; Broman *et al.*, 1975; Knobloch & Pasamanick, 1953). The similar pattern of precocity of urban United States black infants and rural African infants would seem to reduce the efficacy of a cultural argument to explain the phenomenon.

Navajo infants have been reported to be somewhat retarded in motor development, an observation that has been attributed to the cradleboard but that may reflect gene-pool differences. The latter explanation is particularly interesting in light of Freedman's (1975) report of the flaccid muscle tone and paucity of lower limb reflexes in Navajo newborns.

Several other reports of behavioral differences among newborns from different populations are suggestive of gene-pool differences (Brazelton, Robey, & Collier, 1969; Freedman, 1975), although prenatal differences are not easily ruled out. In a particularly well-designed study, Freedman and Freedman (1969) did show differences between small samples of Chinese–American and Caucasian–American newborns whose mothers were members of the same Kaiser-Permanente hospital group. Presumably, many possible differences in prenatal life could be ruled out as competitive hypotheses.

There are few comparable studies of infant mental or language development cross-culturally. We do not know when object permanence or first words first appear in various groups; a first step toward studies of canalization at a population level should certainly include the simple description of the existing group variation.

Whither Studies of Canalization?

Hypotheses about the strong canalization of infant development at species, population, or individual levels have not been thoroughly investigated as yet. The existing evidence from cross-cultural studies suggests that there are variations among groups in the rates of infant development. The origins of these differences are possibly cultural in part and probably genetic in part. Further studies at a descriptive level would clarify the degree of variation among groups in developmental patterns. Studies of infants from two gene pools, some of whom were reared by members of their own culture and compared to others adopted into families of a different group, would clarify the roles of genetic and environmental differences among groups. If canalization is strong for infant development in both groups, then rearing conditions should not affect the differences among infants from different gene pools nor the similarities among infants from the same gene pool. Opportunities for such studies exist, as in the cases of black and Asian infants adopted into Caucasian families from the United States. Is their rate of infant development similar to Caucasian infants in the same families or to infants from the same gene pool reared by members of their own group?

Studies of canalization at an individual level can benefit from several research strategies. Adoptive studies also provide a useful technique to examine the influence of shared genotypes and shared environments. Comparisons of infants with their biological parents can be made for groups reared by their own parents and others reared by adoptive families. Further family studies of siblings and half-siblings, reared together and apart, would enhance our knowledge of genotypic differences in development. An ingenious natural experiment has been devised by one of my former students, Karen Fischer. She is studying the families of adult monozygotic (MZ) twins. In the family constellations are MZ twins, siblings, parents and their children, half-siblings, and separated "parent"–child pairs (composed of the MZ twin with the cotwin's children). The beautiful part of her design is the intactness and normality of the families, who are related in all of those varied ways.

High heritabilities of infant development within a population would suggest that the environments sampled were functionally equivalent and that genotypic differences were important sources of variation. This would be evidence for the canalization of that development within the context of average infant environments. Current evidence from twin and sibling studies of mental development leaves this model in doubt, however, even for the one population studied. There is even less evidence available for the canalization of mental development at a population level.

What we need are better theoretical models, based securely on evolutionary theory. Analysis of variance is the most adequate analytic tool presently available. Data on sources of differences can lead to inferences about canalization at individual and even population levels, but variance models do not inform us directly of the ways in which genes combine with environments to produce development. Ethological studies at the species and population levels are largely descriptive. They seldom inform us of the genetic mechanisms and critical features of the environment that contribute to adaptational variation within the human species. Perhaps, an integration of ethological, biometrical, and Mendelian models can inform us about the causes of developmental canalization in human behaviors with evolutionary significance (Thiessen, 1972). Presently, however, we must test our determinant models with evidence on sources of variation. Let us restrict our claims to empirically appropriate, modest ones that reflect our profound ignorance about the causes of development.

REFERENCES

Bayley, N. Comparisons of mental and motor test scores for ages 1–15 months by sex, birth order, race, geographical location, and education of parents. *Child Development,* 1965, **36,** 379–411.

Benzer, S. Genetic dissection of behavior. *Scientific American,* 1973, **229,** 24–37.

Brazelton, T. B., Robey, J. S., & Collier, G. A. Infant development in the Zincanteco Indians of southern Mexico. *Pediatrics,* 1969, **44,** 274–293.

Broman, S. H., Nichols, P. L., & Kennedy, W. A. *Preschool IQ: Prenatal and early developmental correlates.* Hillsdale, New Jersey: Lawrence Erlbaum Assoc., 1975.

Dennis, W. Causes of retardation among institutional children: Iran. *Journal of Genetic Psychology,* 1960, **96,** 47–59.

Dilger, W. C. The behavior of lovebirds. *Scientific American,* 1962, **206,** 88–98.

Dobzhansky, T. On types, genotypes, and the genetic diversity in populations. In J. Spuhler (Ed.), *Genetic diversity and human behavior.* Chicago: Aldine, 1967. Pp. 1–18.

Dobzhansky, T. *Genetic diversity and human equality.* New York: Basic Books, 1973.

Falconer, D. S. *Introduction to quantitative genetics.* New York: Ronald Press, 1960.

Freedman, D. G. *Human infancy: An evolutionary perspective.* Hillsdale, New Jersey; Lawrence Erlbaum Assoc., 1975.

Freedman, D. G., & Freedman, N. C. Behavioral differences between Chinese–American and European–American newborns. *Nature,* 1969, **24,** 1227.

Freedman, D. G., & Keller, B. Inheritance of behavior in infants. *Science,* 1963, **140,** 196–198.

Geber, M. The psychomotor development of African children in the first year, and the influence of maternal behavior. *Journal of Social Psychology,* 1958, **47,** 185–195.

Ginsburg, B. F. Genetic parameters in behavioral research. In J. Hirsh (Ed.), *Behavior-genetic analysis.* New York: McGraw-Hill, 1967.

Gottesman, I. I. Genetic aspects of intelligent behavior. In N. Ellis (Ed.), *Handbook of mental deficiency.* New York: McGraw-Hill, 1963. Pp. 253–296.

Hebb, D. O. A return to Jensen and his social science critics. *American Psychologist,* 1970, **25** (6), 568.

Kagan, J., & Klein, R. E. Cross-cultural perspectives on early development. *American Psychologist,* 1973, **28,** 947–961.

Knobloch, H., & Pasamanick, B. Further observations on the behavioral development of Negro children. *The Journal of Genetic Psychology,* 1953, **83,** 137–157.

Lehrman, D. Semantic and conceptual issues in the nature-nurture problem. In L. R. Aronson, E. Tobach, & E. Shaw (Eds.), *Development and evolution of behavior.* San Francisco: Freeman, 1970. Pp. 12–25

Lenneberg, E. *Biological foundations of language.* New York: Wiley, 1967.

Lewis, M., & McGurk, H. Evaluation of infant intelligence. *Science,* 1972, **178,** 1174–1177.

Lipsitt, L. P. Discussion of paper by Harris. In E. Tobach, L. R. Aronson, & E. Shaw (Eds.), *The biopsychology of development.* New York: Academic Press, 1971. Pp. 498–501.

Mayr, E. *Populations, species, and evolution.* An abridgment of *Animal species and evolution.* Cambridge, Mass.: The Belknap Press of Harvard University Press, 1970.

McCall, R. B. IQ pattern over age: Comparisons among siblings and parent–child pairs. *Science,* 1970, **170,** 644–648.

McCall, R. B. Similarity in IQ profile among related pairs. *Proceedings, of the 80th Annual Convention, American Psychological Association,* 1972. (a)

McCall, R. B. Similarity in developmental profile among related pairs. *Science,* 1972, **178,** 1004–1005. (b)

McCall, R. B., Appelbaum, M. I., & Hogarty, P. S. Developmental changes in mental performance. *Monographs of the Society for Research in Child Development,* 1973, **38**(3, Whole No. 150).

Piaget, J. *The origins of intelligence in children.* New York: International Universities Press, 1952.

Piaget, J., & Inhelder, B. The gaps in empiricism. In A. Koestler & J. R. Smythies (Eds.), *Beyond reductionism.* Boston: Beacon Press, 1969.

Pick, A. D. Culture and perception. In E. C. Carterette, & M. P. Friedman (Eds.), *Handbook of perception.* New York: Academic Press, 1976 (in press).

Revusky, S. Review of R. A. Hinde & J. Stevenson-Hinde (Eds.), *Constraints on learning: Limitations and predispositions. Contemporary Psychology,* 1974, **19,** 692–694.

Rothenbuhler, W. C. Genetic and evolutionary considerations of social behavior of honeybees and some related insects. In J. Hirsh (Ed.), *Behavior-genetic analysis.* New York: McGraw-Hill, 1967. Pp. 61–111.

Sameroff, A. J., & Chandler, M. J. Reproductive risk and the continuum of caretaking casualty. In F. D. Horowitz, M. Hetherington, S. Scarr-Salapatek, & G. Siegel (Eds.), *Review of child development research.* Vol. 4. Chicago, University of Chicago Press, 1975.

Scarr-Salapatek, S. The effects of early stimulation on low-birth-weight infants. *Child Development,* 1973, **44,** 94–101.

Sperry, R. W. How a developing brain gets itself properly wired for adaptive function. In E. Tobach, L. R. Aronson, & E. Shaw (Eds.), *The biopsychology of development.* New York: Academic Press, 1971. Pp. 27–44.

Stott, L. H., & Ball, R. S. Infant and preschool mental tests: Review and evaluation. *Monographs of the Society for Research in Child Development,* 1965, **30** (Whole No. 101).

Thiessen, D. *Gene organization and behavior.* New York: Random House, 1972.

Wachs, T. Technical comment. *Science,* 1972, **178,** 1005.

Waddington, C. H. Concepts of development. In E. Tobach, L. R. Aronson, & E. Shaw (Eds.), *The biopsychology of development.* New York: Academic Press, 1971. Pp. 17–23.

Warren, N. African infant precocity. *Psychological Bulletin,* 1972, **78,** 353–367.

Werner, H. *Comparative psychology of mental development.* New York: Science Editions, 1961.

Weiss, P. *Dynamics of development: Experiments and inferences.* New York: Academic Press, 1968.

Willerman, L., Broman, S. H., & Fiedler, M. Infant development, preschool IQ, and social class. *Child Development,* 1970, **41,** 69–77.

Wilson, R. S. Twins: Early mental development. *Science,* 1972, **175,** 914–917. (a)

Wilson, R. S. Similarity in developmental profile among related pairs of human infants. *Science,* 1972, **178,** 1005–1007. (b)

Wilson, R. S. & Harpring, E. B. Mental and motor development in infant twins. *Developmental Psychology,* 1972, **7,** 277–287.

Comments on "Genetic Determinants of Infant Development: An Overstated Case"

Philip R. Zelazo

Scarr-Salapatek evaluates the research on infancy to determine the degree to which infant behavioral development can be said to be canalized or genetically limited to a few possible phenotypes. She concludes that we know precious little about the causes of development and suggests that those of biological persuasion temper their strong claims about the genetic bases of development, particularly mental development. Her argument that the proponents of the genetic view have overstated their case is well taken. However, it probably applies equally to the proponents of the environmental position. The sad truth is that we know too little and are claiming too much.

The data on mental development in infants are as inconclusive as the results on IQ and social class in older children (Allen & Pettigrew, 1973; Erlenmeyer-Kimling & Stern, 1973; Scarr-Salapatek, 1973). Moreover, not only are our models limited, as Scarr-Salapatek suggests, but we should perhaps be asking other questions. It appears that in the absence of sound empirical data there may be a tendency to resolve the uncertainty surrounding this issue by substituting our beliefs for facts. Admittedly, it is difficult to tell society, and especially those directly affected by our discoveries and pronouncements, that we must reserve judgment until the facts are in. If we are to avoid making unsubstantiated and perhaps erroneous proclamations with potentially great consequences, however, that is the responsible course to follow.

STATISTICAL AND RESEARCH DESIGN LIMITATIONS

Scarr-Salapatek's evaluation of the limitations of the data on infant mental development reveal that most exising research is observational and correlational. The models that are used most frequently measure sources of variation on a particularly complex trait—intelligence. Yet, it is commonly accepted that observational and correlational procedures represent only a beginning research effort. The chief liability of correlational studies is precisely that they cannot reveal causal determinants. An experimental approach to the study of infant development is possible and desirable. It is commonly acepted that an analysis of variance model, although not perfect for developmental research, offers some important advantages not inherent in a correlational approach; tentative causal statements, examination of multiple independent variables, and a determination of how these variables interact can all be specified. It seems imperative that more short-term longitudinal experimental research be encouraged in this area. There is no reason why children of similar genetic stock, some of whom are placed for adoption and reared in different environments, cannot be recruited to fit a reasonably sound research design.

It is desirable to provide a relatively rigorous examination of environmental influences on mental development, preferably with socioeconomic levels of adoptive parents and sex differences among children controlled. There is a clear need for the controlled examination of cognitive, verbal, and motor development following a marked discontinuity in the child's life from a marginal to a highly favorable environment and executed in a serious, comprehensive, and long-term manner. This quasi-experimental design can be arranged using adoptive children and families. The comprehensive effort inherent in adoption may reveal the extent to which environmental factors can modify performance when the genetic contribution is randomized. The adoption strategy can also permit rigorous research without creating major ethical problems.

Scarr-Salapatek suggests that the adoption strategy offers a reasonable vehicle to test cultural differences in rates of development—a test of canalization at the species level. For example, adoption of African or Asian infants by United States Caucasian families allows for a comparison of mental and motor development with matched Caucasian infants and infants from the same genetic background reared in their own country. This approach not only represents a clever use of a naturally occurring situation but is a practical suggestion for improving the quality of the data.

INADEQUACY OF EXISTING MEASURES

The limitations of research on mental development in children are particularly severe during the first 2 years of life where the measures show little predictive relation to later development (Bayley, 1966; Lewis &

McGurk, 1972; Stott & Ball, 1965). Some researchers have suggested that the low correlations between infant tests and later IQ are a result of different spurts and lags in the genetic blueprint (Wilson, 1972; Wilson & Harpring, 1972), whereas others have suggested that the skills tested vary from age to age, implying different manifestations of intelligence with age (Bayley, 1966; McCall, Appelbaum, & Hogarty, 1973; Stott & Ball, 1965). Whatever the reason, most researchers agree that the relations across age are tenuous. One logical but rarely raised implication of the poor predictive validity is that current tests of infant mental development may fail to measure underlying cognitive processes. It may be that, contrary to most expectations, the items presently used in tests of infant mental development, which are heavily motor and social in appearance and presumed to reflect cognitive abilities either directly or indirectly, may simply not be valid expressions of cognitive ability. Among other things, the poor relation between infant tests and subsequent IQ measures raises doubts about the assumption of sensorimotor intelligence in infancy. The impressive exception to the poor performance among current procedures—the relation between vocalization items in infancy and later verbal IQ in girls (Cameron, Livson, & Bayley, 1967; McCall, Hogarty, & Hurlburt, 1972) —offers partial support for this suggestion. The practical consequences for the debate about genetic and environmental determinants of mental development is that proponents of both sides may have relied on measures of motor and social development that may be orthogonal to cognitive ability.

Cognitive measures free from reliance on motor performance are practically nonexistent. Yet, theoretically and logically they bear the closest relation to later intelligence measures. The hypothesis that infant mental development can be tested without a reliance on gross motor performance is testable and consistent with recent findings. Research during the last decade has shown unequivocally that infants in the first year of life can process and respond to visual, auditory, olfactory, and tactual information without reliance on motor actions. Why then do we cling to the assumption that cognitive development is necessarily predicted through early motor performance? The direct assessment of cognitive development in infants has been limited, among other things, by the absence of a theory that is free from motor constraints to guide the selection of items for infant tests.

The assessment of mental and motor performance in infants has also been hampered by an absence of research on the meanings of infant responses. The knowledge gained from recent investigations of visual fixation, smiling, vocalizing, and heart rate changes allow reasonable hypotheses about infant reactions to specific events, yet this information has generally not been incorporated into existing tests. For example, few of us would dispute that an infant's attention to a repeated event followed by habituation of his looking time indicates that he has at least a partial memory for that event. If we observed smiling (and so recognition) to the repetition of the event before habituation occurred, we would be even more certain that the infant formed an internal representation. It is a straightforward task to test an infant's capacity to form a memory for an event and to measure his reaction to departures from that stimulus. The direct assessment of infant cognitive development could begin with a profile of an infant's capacity to process and store information and to assimilate moderate changes from a standard, a capacity analogous to elementary problem solving.

The logic for a direct assessment of infant cognitive processing is sound and the hypothesis testable. Preliminary data from such an attempt (Zelazo, Kagan, & Hopkins, 1976) show that infants under 1 year of age do indeed attend to visual and auditory events lasting as long as 4 min each. Moreover, the results show reliable differences among children over age and sex on numerous dependent measures to the repetition and moderate change of an event.

However, until such procedures have been tested and their validity established, it is premature to draw convincing conclusions about either genetic or environmental determinants of mental development. Moreover, the validity of current assessment procedures for cognitive development is too tenuous to merit heavy investment in the conclusions derived from their use.

DIFFERENT QUESTIONS AND NEW MODELS

Scarr-Salapatek emphasizes a point that is often overlooked: Common environments may canalize development as much as common genotypes. Similar development produced by such divergent contributions accentuates the difficulty inherent in the study of genetic variability. A shift in emphasis to the study of genetic determination may prove more productive. Moreover, the study of genetic mechanisms associated with behavioral development may be more manageable if a larger, more observable unit than the gene is examined.

In the long run, the study of genetic determination may lead to more productive solutions about behavioral and biological development than the study of genetic variability. The basic question is not whether there is greater or lesser canalization of intellectual development, for example, but for which specific cognitive capacities. Some facets of cognitive development, such as memory span, may be highly canalized and may approach maximum capacity at a very early age, as an admittedly limited, but controlled, observation with a single 3-year-old child and two adults implies.

The task of remembering which containers concealed a particular object, when three, then four, then five different containers and objects were used, was performed equally well by the 3-year-old and the adults. If this observation were to be confirmed with a larger sample, it would reveal relatively early maturation of a specific and fundamental cognitive capacity and would imply that different cognitive abilities inherent in complex intellectual behavior varied in degree of canalization. It appears that the capacity for memory may be highly canalized and develop automatically, in contrast to another cognitive task, such as reading ability, which requires considerable instruction.

Highly canalized behaviors, such as the ability to create cognitive representations of our experiences—to form a memory, to assimilate ideas, to retrieve information, and to speak, may be analogous to reflexes at a motor level. These capacities appear to be highly canalized genetic characteristics of the species, but they are more readily studied than genes. In other words, a more productive emphasis for researchers may be to investigate the reflexive units, both cognitive and motor, with respect to their genetic and environmental limitations. Our reflexive components represent highly canalized behaviors reflecting strong genetic determination, but at a level intermediate to the practically unapproachable genes, on the one end, and experientially acquired complex behaviors, on the other.

Reflexive units, such as the stepping response, are clearly tied to genes and somewhat modifiable through experience; but although we cannot alter the specific gene controlling this response, we can observe and manipulate the walking reflex. Moreover, the acceleration paradigm provides a direct means for the experimental study of reflexes. Scarr-Salapatek's doubts notwithstanding, most of the existing efforts at accelerating development are generally not guided by the belief that faster is better. The advantage of acceleration efforts is that they represent a more benign approach for studying the mechanisms of a developing system than deprivation studies. Facilitation of a system often occurs through efficient use of the system, thereby providing experimental information about its normal functioning. The experimental investigation of reflexive units may not only shed light on larger segments of behavior, therefore, but may provide clues about our genetic organization.

This renewed emphasis on reflexive behaviors may require a final comment. Behavioristic psychology has been obsessed with reflexes in the past; why should we follow that course again? It is paradoxical, that although reflexive behaviors have been widely researched, we know very little about their role in human development. We not only have misconceptions about individual reflexive units, such as the stepping, placing, and standing reflexes in human infants, but we have rarely studied their organization and integration—an exciting enterprise as summarized by

Easton (1972). A study of reflexive behavior in infants may provide evidence to document or clarify the assumption of cephalocaudal development—a belief that has thoroughly influenced our view of early motor development including our tests of infant development. An equally important issue concerns the explication of the process by which cortical inhibition of reflexes occurs. We may ask empirically what the relation is between motor and mental development in infancy—a question of direct consequence for the assessment of infant development.

Answers to these central questions can be produced from renewed research interest in reflexive behavior. Moreover, their resolution will also provide data for the larger question concerning genetic differences. Thus, although few psychologists would deny that the human infant comes into the world with a complex set of reflexive units in virtually every area of his psysiological constitution, few have studied the relevance of these units for the infant's behavioral development. Early behavioristic psychologists may have inadvertently deflected us from this course by emphasizing the classical association of neutral stimuli to reflexive responses. When it became clear that classical conditioning had to be stretched too far to account for much of our complex behavior, we lost interest in the reflexive unit. The suggestion that some behaviors may evolve from reflexive to instrumental actions may serve as a limited corrective. Those behaviors that are crucial to man's basic survival may be highly canalized and one mechanism for expression (and relatively easy study) may be the reflexive pattern—both motor and cognitive.

The approaches to the study of genetic and environmental determinants of infant development can and perhaps should take many directions. Questions about genetic determination are fundamental to questions of genetic differences and should perhaps share a greater portion of the current research effort.

REFERENCES

Allen, G., & Pettigrew, K. D. Technical comment: Heritability of IQ by social class: Evidence inconclusive. *Science,* 1973, **182,** 1042–1044.

Bayley, N. Psychological development of the child, Part III: Mental measurement. In F. Falkner (Ed.), *Human development.* Philadelphia: Saunders, 1966. Pp. 397–407.

Cameron, J., Livson, N., & Bayley, N. Infant vocalizations and their relationship to mature intelligence. *Science,* 1967, **157,** 331–333.

Easton, T. A. On the normal use of reflexes. *American Scientist,* 1972, **60,** 591–599.

Erlenmeyer-Kimling, L., & Stern, S. E. Technical comment: Heritability of IQ by social class: Evidence inconclusive. *Science,* 1973, **182,** 1044–1045.

Lewis, M., & McGurk, H. Evaluation of infant intelligence. *Science,* 1972, **178,** 1174–1177.

McCall, R. B., Appelbaum, M. I., & Hogarty, P. S. Developmental changes in mental performance. *Monographs of the Society for Research in Child Development,* 1973, **38**(3, Whole No. 150).

McCall, R. B., Hogarty, P. S., & Hurlburt, N. Transitions in infant sensorimotor development and the prediction of childhood IQ. *American Psychologist,* 1972, **27,** 728–748.

Scarr-Salapatek, S. Technical comment: Heritability of IQ by social class: Evidence inconclusive. *Science,* 1973, **182,** 1045–1047.

Stott, L. H., & Ball, R. S. Infant and preschool mental tests: Review and evaluation. *Monographs of the Society for Research in Child Development,* 1965, **30** (Whole No. 101).

Wilson, R. S. Twins: Early mental development. *Science,* 1972, **175,** 914–917.

Wilson, R. S., & Harpring, E. B. Mental and motor development in infant twins. *Developmental Psychology,* 1972, **7,** 277–287.

Zelazo, P. R., Kagan, J., & Hopkins, J. R. The exploration of procedures for the assessment of infant cognitive development. In preparation, 1976.

4

From Reflexive to Instrumental Behavior

Philip R. Zelazo

Tufts University School of Medicine

Professionals responsible for advising parents about childcare have long known that the persistence of certain reflexive behaviors in infants is often evidence of neurological damage. Normally many of the infant's integrative reflexes diminish or disappear within the first 10 or 12 months of life. The walking reflex diminishes to near zero by 8 weeks (Zelazo, Zelazo, & Kolb, 1972) and the Moro reflex terminates by about 6 months (McGraw, 1943). The occurrence of a full-fledged Moro reflex in an 10-month-old child, arms extended and brought toward the midline with grasping of the hands, to the sudden removal of support, may therefore raise concern about the infant's neurological status. This concern rests on a firm foundation of clinical experience; in some cases of neurological insult, the so-called integrative reflexes, such as the Moro reflex, persist or reappear.

Generalizations are occasionally made to less obvious cases, however, implying that the persistence or reoccurrence of certain reflexes beyond prescribed ages is synonymous with abnormal development. One obvious implication, voiced even today, is that we should not tamper with any of the infant's reflexes. Some suggest that the presence of reflexively based responses beyond certain ages, such as walking or standing in the 2-month-old infant, is cause for concern (e.g., Gotts, 1972). This is a reasonable view if one regards the infant as a defenseless organism. There is a sense of security that accompanies alignment with prevailing child-rearing procedures. In a situation bearing some uncertainty the current dominant practice in our society of providing the infant relatively little opportunity for the exercise of his full reflexive repertoire appears safe.

Proponents of this view suggest that the infant's reflexive behaviors normally disappear and are eventually replaced by voluntary actions. For example, in discussing the development of voluntary eye–hand coordination Bruner and Bruner (1968) argue that ". . . before programmed voluntary action can get underway, . . . there must first be a recession of reflex control over the acts that are governed by a program [252]." They acknowledge the precise reflex components described by Twitchell (1970)—shoulder–traction grasping, the touch-evoked grasp reflex, touch-evoked avoidance–withdrawal, pronating and supinating groping without visual guidance—but state flatly that ". . . in no sense are these the paving blocks from which skilled programs of visually guided action are constructed [252]." A corollary of this position is that the infant is defenseless in the presence of those stimuli which may initiate his reflexes. Higher order control cannot occur until some later age when neurological maturation permits the emergence of a new voluntary system. However, Twitchell (1970) claims that "although it is commonly stated that infantile reflexes disappear during maturation, we have shown that this is an erroneous impression [p. 36]." Indeed, current behavioral and neurological research with infants challenges the validity and generality of the hypothesized independence between early reflexive and later instrumental behavior.

An alternative hypothesis holds that the newborn's reflexes do not disappear but retain their identity within a hierarchy of controlled behavior. This view holds that with use the child develops the capacity to control his reflexive actions and that the reflexive components are incorporated into a smoother, less stereotyped system. A corollary of this position is that with use the child develops the capacity to inhibit, as well as activate, the reflexive components. The infant's refusal to eat, as most mothers have seen, and his failure to walk each time he is stimulated, implies that he is not defenseless even during the neonatal period. Andre-Thomas (Andre-Thomas & Autgaerden, 1966), a French neurologist who studied infant locomotion extensively, including the stepping reflex, wrote about the difficulty in eliciting one particular reflexive pattern of behavior in infants:

> The newborn is capricious and does not always walk to order. Well disposed one moment, he is no longer so the next. The examiner is discouraged and gives up; then he changes his mind and tries a last time—the baby starts walking immediately, perfectly regularly and over a long distance. Even though attempts to elicit primary walking fail repeatedly, the possibility is still there. At ten o'clock he may not walk but a few seconds later he may [pp. 2–3].

Although it is not clear why the connection between the unconditioned stimulus and the unconditioned response is not automatic, it is clear that the infant is not simply at the mercy of a single unconditioned stimulus that produces an automatic invariant reaction. It is also likely that the infant's reflexes do not disappear but come under higher central nervous system control.

Easton (1972) cites recent biological research with human and infrahuman aldults that implies that many, if not most, complex adult volitional motor responses may incorporate basic reflexive components. There appears to be a phylogenetic progression in cortical control of reflexive behavior; higher levels of CNS involvement in reflexive actions are shown for humans than for monkeys, who in turn show higher level CNS involvement than cats. All three species show more reliance on higher CNS functioning in the elicitation of reflexive behavior than the rat. Easton's evaluation of research on reflexive responding in animals with decerebrate preparations led him to conclude that ". . . the more CNS tissue there is below the level of section and connected to the musculature, the more complex, accurate, and appropriate the motor repertoire elicitable from an animal [p. 592]." For example, animals with a decerebrate split at the spinal level may show extreme rigidity, whereas animals with a higher level preparation may show standing and stepping.

Easton also presents data indicating complex reflexive involvement in coordinated motor behavior in normal adults. For example, work by Hellebrandt and his associates (Hellebrandt, Houtz, Partridge, & Walters, 1956; Hellebrandt, Schade, & Carns, 1962) indicates that the tonic neck reflex may be activated to facilitate volitional effort. The task of lifting a load either by extension or flexion of the wrist could be facilitated or inhibited by the voluntary elicitation of the tonic neck reflex. Whether elicited voluntarily or spontaneously, a supportive tonic neck pattern resulted in increased work output. These results led Easton (1972) to suggest that the CNS may ". . . compose volitional movements out of reflexes and complex reflexes out of simpler ones, that, when the command lines to the component reflexes of a movement are saturated by effort or fatigue and more effort is required the appropriate level of the CNS may call upon other reflexes . . . [p. 593]." To support his suggestion of higher order control of coordinated reflexes Easton observes that the tuning reflexes, such as the tonic neck reflexes, may be influenced by perceptual–cognitive factors. The tonic neck reflex prejudices movement toward the organism's direction of visual gaze, for example. A change in attention may elicit a tonic neck reflex that permits a complex adjustment in direction without altering the organization of reflexes involved. In summary, these data imply that reflexes operate in the coordination of motor behavior in normal, intact, healthy organisms, including adult humans. The results support the notion that reflexive components do not disappear but instead come under higher order control—a view that is both theoretically parsimonious and consistent with physiological evidence. Viewed in this way, the reflexes are analogous to the modular components used in the construction of prefabricated houses.

Jean Piaget (1952) is perhaps the most prominent theorist to suggest that the infant's first competences—sucking, rooting, and grasping, for example—are reflexive and only gradually get integrated into a complex coordinated action. He suggests that when an infant reaches for an object, brings it to his mouth, and sucks on it, he is demonstrating the coordination and integration of individual and initially separate reflexes. Piaget has argued that "the reflex must be conceived as an organized totality whose nature it is to preserve itself by functioning and consequently to function sooner or later for its own sake (repetition) while incorporating into itself objects propitious to this functioning (generalized assimilation) and discerning situations necessary to certain special modes of its activity (motor recognition) [p. 38]." Reflexes are therefore presumed to develop into coordinated voluntary actions through adaptation to the environment.

This view has gained support from research on learning in infants. In one of the first rigorous demonstrations of the modifiability of reflexive behavior in newborns, Lipsitt and Kaye (1965) showed that newborns could adapt their reflexive sucking to changes in nipple shape. Three groups of neonates were given either an ordinary bottle nipple, a piece of straight ¼-inch rubber laboratory tubing, or alternation between the rubber tubing and the nipple. Observers recorded the number of sucks during a total of 50 trials lasting 10 sec each. The results revealed that the bottle nipple elicited more sucking that the tube, confirming earlier observations that different stimuli have different capacities for eliciting sucking in newborns. The more important result, however, occurred in the alternation condition, where sucking to the nipple was less than in the nipple-alone condition and increased over blocks of trials. Sucking to the tube, in contrast, started somewhat higher than the tube-alone condition and decreased over blocks of trials. Neonates receiving alternating blocks of trials therefore showed increasing sucking to the nipple and decreasing sucking to the tube, indicating that neonatal sucking is influenced by prior experience. This experimental demonstration of the modification or adaptation of reflexive sucking during the first days of life led to a number of convincing demonstrations that the infant is in direct commerce with his environment as recipient and initiator of action from the first moments of life.

Researchers at Brown University—Lipsitt, Siqueland, and Eimas—have demonstrated convincingly that reflexive responding in infants, in this case sucking, can come under instrumental (or operant) control. Lipsitt (1971a) has established that young infants will suck to produce movement in a mobile. Siqueland (1969) has shown that 1-month-old babies will suck to control the presentation of colorful slides, and Eimas, Siqueland, Jusczyk, and Vigorito (1971) have used a similar operant procedure with auditory stimuli to show that infants can reliably discriminate the phonemes /p/ and /b/ at 4 weeks of age. The presentation of a colorful slide or a simple sound immediately following each suck serves as feedback or as a reward in the operant paradigm. This form of eliciting a reflexive response is distinct from a situation where an unconditioned stimulus (for example, nipple in the baby's mouth) is presented alone or where a neutral stimulus (for example, a bell) is presented prior to the unconditioned stimulus until the neutral stimulus gains the capacity to elicit the reflex. In the operant paradigm, control over a response occurs through following the desired response with a reward. It has become increasingly clear from these and other data (e.g., Sameroff, 1972) that operant conditioning is more readily demonstrated in early infancy than classical conditioning and that the greatest success appears to occur with the operant control of reflexive responses.

Lipsitt (1971b) has recently suggested that it may be necessary to exercise and reinforce, either naturally or deliberately, some reflexes or congenital patterns of behavior for favorable development to occur. This hypothesis is consistent with research on the newborn walking reflex (Zelazo, Zelazo, & Kolb, 1972), which shows that exercise of the walking response increases the frequency of occurrence. Some reflexive patterns that are congenitally weak or fail to get stimulated and become difficult to elicit may place the infant in jeopardy if those responses are vital to his survival. Lipsitt suggests that the congenital pattern of behavior elicited through respiratory occlusion may be one response pattern that enables the infant to prevent his own suffocation. For example, if a neonate's mouth and nostrils are occluded with a gauze pad, he usually responds by turning from side to side, thrusting his head backwards, grimacing and flushing and eventually by bringing his arms toward his face in swiping motions and crying. Placing the gauze over the mouth and nose area without holding it there appears to result in increasingly more efficient hand swiping and removal of the obstructing pad. Practice in removeing occluding stimuli appears to occur naturally in the infant's crib. Lipsitt speculates that some of the 10,000 infants who die each year from the mysterious crib death syndrome may be victims of a weak "fighting reaction" to nasal–oral occlusion. This extremely important and fascinating implication from recent research on the neonatal reflexive repertoire is well founded and deserves immediate research attention.

The notion that infant reflexes may become difficult to elicit if not stimulated gains some support from Gunther's (1961) careful observations of neonatal sucking at the mother's breast. She reported that some babies put to breast do not receive the proper stimulation because of the shape of the breast and do not suck. She also demonstrated that sucking often must be primed and if not exercised very soon after birth may be difficult to elicit. Other infants who experience occlusion of the nostrils while feeding, from having either their own upper lip or the mother's breast pushed against their nostrils, may not only refuse to feed but may cry when turned toward the mother after only two or three experiences. These cautious observations are consistent with the hypothesis that some of the infant's reflexes may require exercise in order to be elicited with ease and that the reflexes may come under higher CNS control sooner than commonly believed.

NEWBORN STEPPING RESEARCH

The instrumental control of gross motor reflexive behavior in the infant was suggested by Myrtle McGraw in 1932. She proposed that some responses occurred on a reflex level before they became part of a controlled muscular pattern. The reflexes appear to diminish before the controlled pattern emerges but the transition is gradual; there is no sudden emergence of a coordinated response. The learning involved in the assumption of an erect posture and walking is described as improvement in the degree and precision of a response rather than the elimination of false responses or the selection of satisfying ones (McGraw, 1932, p. 297). The gradual development from supported reflexive stepping in the newborn to self-supported walking was observed and described.

Experimental intervention was reported in a later publication involving two dizygotic twins (McGraw, 1935). One twin, Johnny, received a long series of exercises to facilitate his motor development beginning at birth. The other twin, Jimmy, served as a control, receiving only limited opportunity to exercise his motor system. Of particular interest here is the fact that Johnny's stepping reflex was stimulated from birth, whereas Jimmy's was not. Unfortunately, the description of the exercises and results received only cursory mention. Nevertheless, McGraw reported that Johnny showed far more stepping than Jimmy, although he did not walk alone sooner.

Andre-Thomas and Autgaerden (1953, 1966) also report the performance of a single child who received daily exercise of the stepping reflex from about the second week of life. The training was carried out by the mother, with tests held at irregular and varying intervals. Nevertheless it was clear from the report that at 3 weeks of age the infant marched ". . . like a trained soldier and so fast that we had to hold him back" [1966, p. 38]. When retested on the thirty-eighth day he was less disposed to walk for the examiners but walked for his mother.

Zelazo, Zelazo, and Kolb (1972) recently demonstrated facilitation of the walking response in neonates through brief daily exercise of the walking reflex using more conventional experimental procedures. One group of 1-week-old infants was given a total of 12 min of exercise each day for 7 weeks. These babies were supported under the arms and the soles of their feet were allowed contact with a flat surface—usually a table top. Walking steps were accompanied by a forward progression in order to encourage alternately stepping responses. A passive exercise control group received comparable social and gross motor stimulation for an equivalent amount of time. These babies were placed in an infant seat or crib and their legs and arms were gently exercised in a pumping motion. All training was conducted by the mothers and testing by the experimenters. A third group received no exercise but was tested each week for 8 weeks along with the active and passive exercise groups. A fourth group served as a control for the possible facilitative effects of repeated examination and was tested only once at 8 weeks of age. All infants were tested when they were judged to be alert and inactive (Wolff, 1959), a condition usually achieved shortly after waking (Papousek, 1967). The number of walking responses to occur during a 1-min test session similar to the training sessions was the major dependent variable.

The results are illustrated in Figure 4.1. Infants given active exercise of the stepping reflex increased their average number of steps during testing from about eight before training to almost 30 by the eighth week of life. Passive and no-exercise control infants started with 7.8 and 5.4 steps, respectively, and averaged about three responses by the last test session. The 8-week control infants showed the lowest level of stepping, averaging fewer than one step. This decline in stepping to near zero appeared to confirm observations that the walking response disappears by about 8

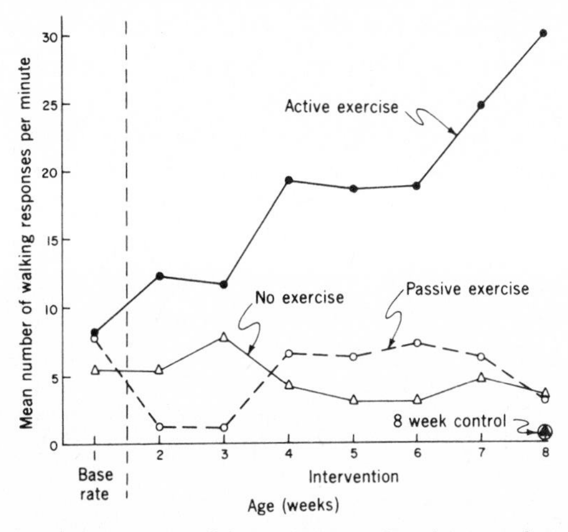

FIGURE 4.1 Mean number of walking responses for the experimental and control groups during the first 8 weeks of life. (From Zelazo, Zelazo, & Kolb, 1972.)

weeks and implied a possible critical period for exercising the walking response.

The most parsimonious interpretation of the increase among active exercise infants that is consistent with existing research on learning is that stepping was transformed from a predominantly reflexive to an instrumental response—that instrumental learning occurred. Although stepping was initially elicited by an unconditioned stimulus, it appears that the increase in responding was produced by the rewarding consequences of walking—presumably the vertical orientation and varied visual stimulation. It is unlikely that the classical conditioning of secondary eliciting stimuli, typically weaker elicitors than the unconditioned stimuli, would produce a linear increase in stepping over the seven weeks of training. The most convincing explanation of the increased stepping that accompanied practice is that instrumental or operant learning occurred. The corresponding changes in brain structure that must accompany the growth from reflexive to instrumental behavior may be explained more adequately by neurologists than by psychologists. The behavioral evidence implies that higher-order control is superimposed on the initial reflexive pattern, perhaps allowing for "voluntary" initiation and inhibition. The identification of the change from reflexive to instrumental processes offers precise behavioral guidelines for exploring the parameters of specific infantile motor patterns. Further behavioral research on the development from reflexive to instrumental control may provide clues for the neurologist and assist him in the construction of more sophisticated models of infant brain structure.

A second experiment conducted with Gary Schwartz and Sara Kolb (Zelazo, Schwartz, & Kolb, in preparation, 1976) attempted to test the critical period hypothesis. It was conjectured that children around the age of disappearance of the reflex would require more time to show increases in responding with equivalent practice or fail to show the response at all. Three groups of infants began 6 weeks of active exercise at 2, 6, and 10 weeks of age. Three control groups received no training and were tested only once each at either 8, 12, or 16 weeks of age, points corresponding to the ends of the training sessions. Procedures were the same as in the first experiment except that (1) exercise occurred for 9 instead of 12 min each day, and (2) the experiment lasted for 6 instead of 7 weeks. Stepping responses were recorded for two 1-min test periods each week and the mean for the 2 min served as the principal dependent variable.

Active exercise produced gradual but consistent increases in walking steps in all three groups as shown in Figure 4.2. Two-week-old infants began with an average of six steps per minute and increased to 12.3 responses by 8 weeks of age, whereas the 8-week control infants averaged under one step. Six-week-old infants displayed about four steps on the first day of testing and increased to a high of 12.2 steps by 12 weeks,

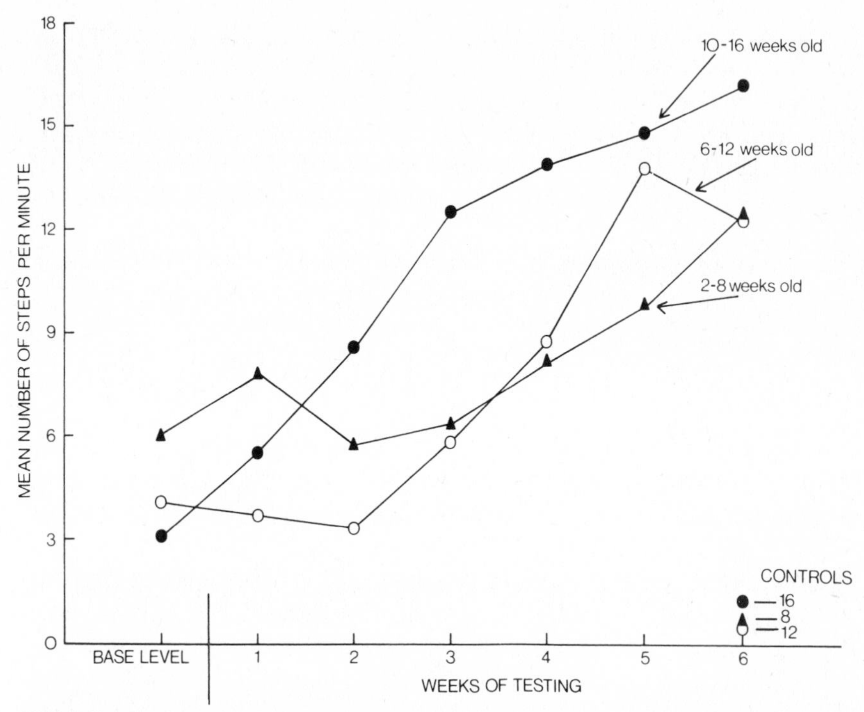

FIGURE 4.2 Mean number of walking responses for 2-, 6-, and 10-week-old infants receiving 6 weeks of exercise and their nonexercised controls. (From Zelazo, Schwartz, & Kolb, 1976, in preparation.)

whereas the corresponding 12-week-old control group averaged only half a step. Infants who began the program at 10 weeks of age averaged three steps per minute on the first day of testing and increased linearly to 16.2 steps by 16 weeks of age. The 16-week-old control group averaged just over one response. These data show that children within the first 4 months of life can learn walking steps if given the opportunity and they support the suggestion that increased walking resulting from practice reflects instrumental learning.

The results also imply that the stepping reflex does not disappear. The production of alternate walking steps represents a complex coordinated event, yet the number of walking responses increased by more than 70% for all active exercise infants except two, despite the fact that no effort was made to "teach" infants to walk. The babies' legs were not lifted in walking motions, their knees were not bent for them, nor were alternate steps primed manually. Infants were held upright, allowed to stand, support their own weight, and step. However, moving the baby forward when he was stepping seemed to encourage alternation. The final level of stepping and the rate of increase for all three active exercise groups was similar, implying that no critical period exists. Comparable learning among groups supports the suggestion that the walking reflex remains intact and that other factors, perhaps incompatible muscular involvement, prevents its elicitation. This view has the advantage of parsimony because it postualates higher cortical control of a programmed unit rather than the disappearance of an existing response with the development of an entirely new system.

POSTURAL INTERFERENCE: OBSERVATIONS OF A SINGLE INFANT

The reduction to near zero in all four no-exercise control groups may be explained by the development of postural or muscular reactions that prevent the proper eliciting conditions (contact between the sole of the foot and a flat surface) from occurring. This situation might be analogous to those neonates described by Gunther (1961) who failed to suck at the breast because the shape of the mother's breast prevented the proper eliciting conditions. We observed that some of the older children failed to extend their legs or support their weight initially and that often their legs and ankles rotated inward. This explanation is illustrated in an extreme case occurring with a single 7½-month-old infant who did not participate in the earlier experiments. This child received an abundance of cognitive and social stimulation and was freely allowed objects for manipulation, but her parents and caretakers rarely permitted her to stand or walk until she approached the "appropriate age." The infant developed a sitting posture with legs extended at right angles to the trunk even when she was suspended under the arms. Two adults gently straightened her posture and gradually encouraged the infant to bear her own weight by supporting her knees and lowering her body weight onto the soles of her feet. This intervention produced no displeasure whatsoever and lasted about 15 min. When the infant seemed able to support her weight, she was held under the arms and given an apportunity to walk. She immediately marched forward and produced more than a dozen high-stepping, unmistakably reflexive responses. Her steps appeared identical to those of a newborn and did not resemble the modulated steps of the older child who achieves upright progression.

This is but a single observation, but the circumstances surrounding this case are both unique and theoretically significant. The relatively easy elicitation of a strong reflexive response at 7½ months of age following specific postural adjustments implies that the reflexive response remains intact despite its apparent disappearance. It is quite certain from parental and caretaker statements and the child's posture that walking was rarely if ever attempted prior to this brief intervention. Walking was encouraged from this day on, reflecting a sharp discontinuity in the treatment of this child. Walking alone occurred at exactly 12 months of age.

THE SIGNIFICANCE OF INFANCY

The research on infancy has produced good evidence that some infant reflexive responses come under instrumental or operant control. This form of learning is neither the exclusive classically conditioned association resulting from the pairing of a neutral stimulus and an unconditioned stimulus described by Pavlov, nor the operant association between a response and a reinforcing condition, such as Skinner defined. This relatively uncommon position holds that reflexive actions are responsive to operant or instrumental control under natural child-rearing situations. This view, proposed by Bijou and Baer (1965) and supported by subsequent research, reflects a contribution to learning theory that has evolved, to a large extent, from research on infants. It makes great sense from an evolutionary point of view that nature should not leave the development of responses that are so important to the infant's survival, such as rooting, sucking, the removal of nasal occlusion, grasping, and stepping, to chance alone. Indeed, Prechtl (1971) argues that infantile behavior patterns enable the newborn to fulfill his vital functions under the normal care of his mother and that his extensive neuromotor repertoire must be viewed in the context of child–mother interaction (Prechtl, 1971, pp. 137–138). Provision of intact reflexive components that come under higher control with use also lends support to Piaget's conception of cognitive development during the early phases of the sensorimotor period.

SMILING: A COGNITIVELY BASED REFLEXIVE RESPONSE

Research on infancy has produced an additional body of data that implies a need to extend our traditional view of reflexive behavior in still another way. A series of experiments shows that smiling occurs when the infant recognizes a stimulus or event, a result consistent with a modification of Piaget's (1952) recognitory assimilation hypothesis (Zelazo, 1972). More specifically, it appears that with repeated presentation of a novel stimulus the infant develops an abstract internal representation of the stimulus (cf. Kagan, 1971; Lewis & Goldberg, 1969; Sokolov, 1963; Zelazo, 1972). This internal representation, called a schema by Kagan (1971), need not be a sensorimotor event as implied by Piaget (1952). Smiling seems to occur only when there is some effort at matching the stimulus to this internal representation. A stimulus that is either too familiar or too novel does not elicit the smile. For example, in one experiment (Zelazo & Komer, 1971) relatively simple but novel sounds (such as an 8-sec segment of "sing a song of sixpence") were repeatedly presented to 3-month-old infants. There were two blocks of trials on two consecutive days. It can be seen in Figure 4.3 that smiling is lowest on the first and last blocks and highest on the two intermediate blocks; the second block of trials on the first day and the first block on the second day have elicited the most smiling. Smiling to the stationary visual stimuli that were also used was equivocal, but the same curvilinear pattern obtained with auditory stimuli has since been demonstrated with sequentially presented visual stimuli (cf. Zelazo, 1972). The point to be made is contained in the auditory curve; the smile, like the walking and grasping reflexes, occurs when a specific set of conditions are met. Effortful matching can occur with numerous stimuli, just as walking can be elicited when the sole of the foot makes contact with numerous surfaces—a table top, a carpeted floor, even a father's chest. However, unlike the other reflexes, the smile

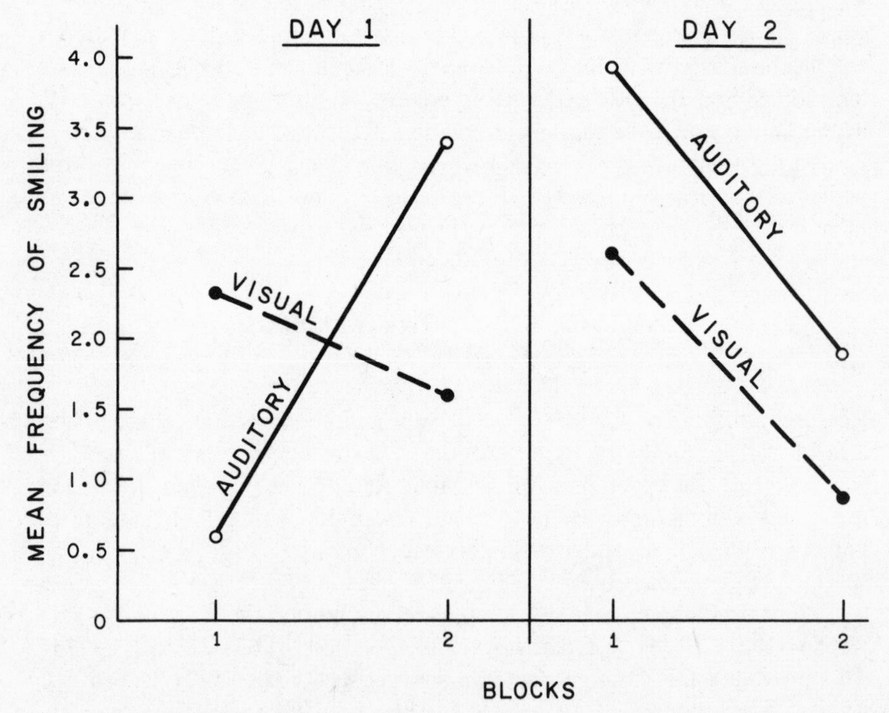

FIGURE 4.3 Mean frequency of smiling to visual and auditory stimuli over trial blocks and days. (From Zelazo & Komer, 1971.)

occurs during a cognitive event—a particular point in the development of the hypothetical schema.

Psychologists have not been quick to view any aspect of cognitive behavior as reflexive and, in fact, the suggestion of a "cognitive reflex" may appear paradoxical. Cognitive behavior and the processing of information tends to be synonomous with volition. This is not to suggest that all cognitive behavior, or even a substantial portion of it, is reflexive; it is to suggest that the smile is ". . . a relatively simple, rapid, and automatic unlearned response . . ." (Kimble & Garmezy, 1968, p. 712) to a specific set of stimulus conditions. No one needs initially to teach the 3-month-old infant to smile to the human face. Moreover, there is additional evidence that smiling, like walking, can eventually come under instrumental control.

In an earlier experiment on the conditionability of the baby's smile to an adult face (Zelazo, 1971) 3-month-old infants were assigned to one of three conditions. One group of infants received immediate smiling, touching, and talking from an adult woman each time they smiled. A second group received an equivalent amount of adult responsiveness but independent of their own smiling. A third group observed a completely unresponsive adult. There were three blocks of 6-min trials presented for 3 consecutive days. The adult remained unresponsive in all three groups on the first day in order to establish a base level; responsiveness occurred on the second and third days. The results are displayed in Figure 4.4. Contingent or immediate responsiveness produced greater smiling on the first conditioning trial block (Day 2) than unresponsiveness or noncontingent responsiveness, indicating that the smile can be instrumentally con-

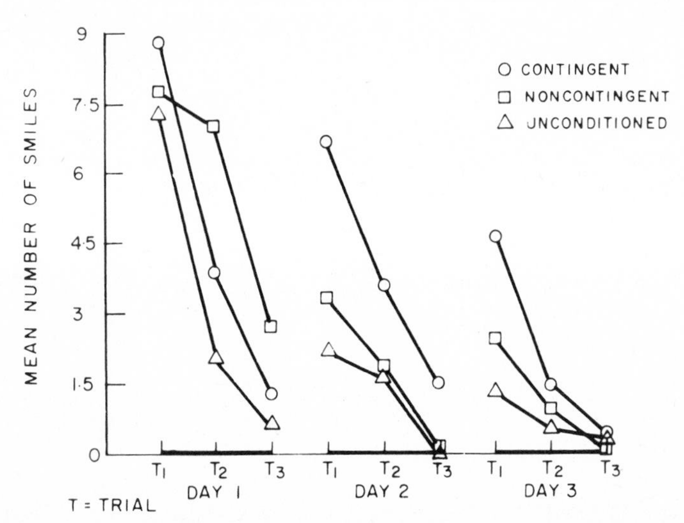

FIGURE 4.4 Mean smiling over trial blocks and days for contingent (○), noncontingent (□) and unconditioned (△) groups of infants. (From Zelazo, 1971.)

ditioned. However, the most prominent result, more characteristic of some reflexive responses (e.g., the orienting response to an auditory signal) is the persistent habituation in all three groups. Presumably, with repetition the initially moderately discrepant face becomes familiar, is more easily recognized, and smiling wanes—even if responsiveness is presented contingently.

IMPLICATIONS

These data on smiling and walking allow interesting speculations. First, even though the behavioral evidence is strong, it has not been shown conclusively that the same reflexive units appearing in the newborn infant's motor repertoire appear in later voluntary actions. It would be especially profitable to examine this development in the infrahuman infant with electromyographic recordings.

Second, perhaps the infant neurological examination should be reconsidered from a behavioral perspective. Might not a better understanding of normal development from reflexive to instrumental behavior permit a refinement of the neurological examination? Can procedures be developed that are more sensitive to subtle neurological deficits than the current presence or absence distinction? The neurological status of the infant is of great consequence to infant and parent. Its investigation is intimately interdisciplinary and in need of collaboration between the neurologist and the psychologist who can bring an improving behavioral methodology and technology to the task. The research discussed earlier, for example, raises questions about the assumption of an invariant cephalocaudal sequence in infant motor development. The infant can stand erect with support, lift his legs when the dorsa of his feet are drawn against an edge, and make alternate marching steps when the soles of his feet touch a flat surface. Each of these responses is as sophisticated as grasping or sucking and each appears as amenable to environmental influence.

Third, we should also question the tests of motor, and indirectly mental, development that are predicted on the assumption of an invariant motor sequence as Myrtle McGraw suggested in the early 1930s. Her concern is as appropriate today as it was then. She asked ". . . why one perfectly normal infant should walk alone at nine months and another not until he is eighteen or twenty months old. . . . Will the one infant walk any better when he is ten years old than the other and does it follow that he will display mental superiority?" (McGraw, 1932, p. 291). What does it mean to include the item "stands up by furniture" at 8.6 months on a test of motor development (Bayley, 1969) when, as can be seen in Figure 4.5, "stands holding on to furniture" can occur at 8 weeks of age? The items are not identical and the phenomenon is unusual, but the question is no less appropriate. The demonstrated modest to low predictive validity of tests of motor development should lead us to question what it is that these widely used scales measure.

Recent observations of San infants in the Kalahari Desert by Melvin Konner (1973, 1976) and of Kipsigis babies in Kenya by Charles Super (1976) show that infant motor precocity for these African babies develops for responses that are practiced by their parents—sitting, standing, and walking, for example. Literally thousands of observations of the stepping response in East African infants from the first weeks of life through the twelfth month reveal that stepping with support under the arms is almost always present in some form. No less than 86% of the children produced stepping at every age of testing during the first year of life, indicating that the stepping response does not disappear when exercised. Super also observed that stepping undergoes a transformation from a high "marching" quality to a modulated, smoother, more mature pattern over the first year.

FIGURE 4.5 An 8-week-old infant standing while holding on to a sofa.

Super (1976) compared Kipsigis babies to the Bayley norms and found that they were "... three to four months precocious on upright progression to walking and other scales involving strength and coordination of the legs. . . ." The number of children tested for "rolling over"—a response that is not practiced—is smaller but the available data indicate that Kipsigis babies develop this ability about 1 month later than infants in the United States. In other words, there was no overall precocity as often suggested (e.g., Geber & Dean, 1957). Kipsigis babies were slightly behind on responses that were less often used and advanced on behaviors that were practiced. Super established through interviews that Kipsigis mothers believe that their babies must be taught to walk and sit, the behaviors in which they show precocity, but need not be taught to roll over or crawl. Home observations are consistent with the interview and assessment data and reveal that Kipsigis infants spend the majority of their waking time seated, or carried on the back or hip, but rarely lying down. Konner (1973) also observed that San parents encourage their infants to stand, step, and bounce.

Solomons and Solomons (1975), recently completed an examination of 288 Yucatecan infants in Mexico and also found specificity in motor precocity. Twelve boys and 12 girls were tested on the Bayley Infant Motor Scale each month from ½ month to 12½ months of age. The results indicated that Yucatecan infants, who are normally carried on the arms or hips displayed excellent prehensile skills and were advanced relative to American norms during the first 9 months. Performance during the end of the first year, when locomotion items dominate the Bayley scale, was reversed. Yucatecan infants scored significantly lower than American infants by 12 months of age, when only 9 of 288 babies walked. The authors report that Yucatecan infants are rarely placed on the floor and appear to get little training in standing and walking. The data from Kipsigis, San, and Yucatecan infants therefore imply that Western norms of motor development may reflect our child-rearing practices rather than the infant's capacities to a greater extent than we previously acknowledged.

Motor development is important in its own right and we should continue to study the interplay between biology and environment in the physical maturation of the infant. However, existing data imply that an alternate route is needed for measuring mental development. Perhaps we should assess the infant's capacity to process information, or to solve simple problems, or to attend to moderate changes in his world, instead of marking the time when the infant's biological program and environmental happenstance interact to produce his first step under his own support or to allow him to pick up a cube deftly and directly.

ACKNOWLEDGMENTS

This research was supported in part by a grant from the Milton Fund, Harvard University. I thank Richard Kearsley for his helpful comments on an earlier draft of this manuscript and Ms. Jean Soo Hoo and Ms. Adrienne Gurevitz, who collaborated in one of the observations.

REFERENCES

Andre-Thomas, & Autgaerden, S. Les deux marches. La marche automatique du nouveau-né, dominance sous-corticale la marche automatique definitive et libérée sous controle cortical: La marche définitive de l'enfant eutrainé quotidiennement. *Presse Medicale,* 1953, **61,** 582–584.

Andre-Thomas, & Autgaerden, S. *Locomotion from pre- to post-natal life.* Lavenham, Suffolk, England: Spastics Society Medical Education and Information Unit, and William Heinemann Medical Books Ltd., 1966.

Bayley, N. *Manual for the Bayley scales of infant development.* New York: The Psychological Corporation, 1969.

Bijou, S. W., & Baer, D. M. *Child development II: Universal stage of infancy.* New York: Appleton-Century-Crofts, 1965.

Bruner, J. S., & Bruner, B. M. On voluntary action and its hierarchical structure. *International Journal of Psychology,* 1968, **3,** 239–255.

Easton, T. A. On the normal use of reflexes. *American Scientist,* 1972, **60,** 591–599.

Eimas, P. D., Siqueland, E. R., Jusczyk, P., & Vigorito, J. Speech perception in infants. *Science,* 1971, **171,** 303–306.

Geber, M., & Dean, R. F. The state of development of newborn African children. *Lancet,* 1957, **1,** 1216–1219.

Gotts, E. E. Newborn walking. *Science,* 1972, **177,** 1057–1058.

Gunther, M. Infant behavior at the breast. In B. M. Foss (Ed.), *Determinants of infant behavior.* Vol. 1. New York: Wiley, 1961. Pp. 37–44.

Hellebrandt, F. A., Houtz, S. J., Partridge, M. J., & Walters, C. E. Tonic neck reflexes in exercises of stress in man. *American Journal of Physical Medicine,* 1956, **35,** 144–159.

Hellebrandt, F. A., Schade, M., & Carns, M. L. Methods of evoking the tonic neck reflexes in normal human subjects. *American Journal of Physical Medicine,* 1962, **41,** 90–139.

Kagan, J. *Change and continuity in infancy.* New York: Wiley, 1971.

Kimble, G. A., & Garmezy, N. *Principles of general psychology.* (3rd ed.) New York: Ronald Press, 1968.

Konner, M. Newborn walking: Additional data. *Science,* 1973, **178,** 307.

Konner, M. Maternal care, infant behavior, and development among the Kalahari Desert San. In R. B. Lee & I. DeVore (Eds.), *Kalahari hunter-gatherers.* Cambridge, Massachusetts: Harvard University Press, 1976. In press.

Lewis, M., & Goldberg, S. The acquisition and violation of expectancy: An experimental paradigm. *Journal of Experimental Child Psychology,* 1969, **7,** 70–80.

Lipsitt, L. P. Infant learning: the blooming, buzzing confusion. In M. E. Meyer (Ed.), *Second western symposium on learning: Early learning.* Bellingham: Western Washington State College, 1971. Pp. 5–21. (a)

Lipsitt, L. P. Infant anger: Toward an understanding of the ontogenesis of human aggression. Unpublished paper presented at the Department of Psychiatry, The Center for the Health Sciences, University of California at Los Angeles, March 4, 1971. (b)

Lipsitt, L. P., & Kaye, H. Change in neonatal response to optimizing and non-optimizing sucking stimulation. *Psychonomic Science,* 1965, **2,** 221–222.

McGraw, M. B. From reflex to muscular control in the assumption of an erect posture and ambulation in the human infant. *Child Development,* 1932, **3,** 291–297.

McGraw, M. B. *Growth, a study of Johnny and Jimmy.* New York: Appleton Century, 1935.

McGraw, M. B. *The neuromuscular maturation of the human infant.* New York: Hafner, 1943.

Papousek, H. Experimental studies of appetitional behavior in human newborns and infants. In H. Stevenson, E. Hess, & H. Rheingold (Eds.), *Early behavior: Comparative and developmental approaches.* New York: Wiley, 1967. Pp. 249–277.

Piaget, J. *The origins of intelligence in children.* New York: International Universities Press, 1952. (French edition, 1936.)

Prechtl, H. F. R. Motor behavior in relation to brain structure. In Stoelinga, v.d. Werfften Bosch (Eds.), *Normal and abnormal development of brain and behavior.* Leiden: Leiden University Press, 1971. Pp. 133–145.

Sameroff, A. Learning and adaptation in infancy: A comparison of models. In H. W. Reese (Ed.), *Advances in child development and behavior.* Vol. 7. New York: Academic Press, 1972. Pp. 170–214.

Siqueland, E. R. The development of instrumental-exploratory behavior during the first year of human life. Paper presented at the meetings of the Society for Research in Child Development, Santa Monica, California, March 1969.

Sokolov, Y. N. *Perception and the conditioned reflex.* New York: Macmillan, 1963.

Solomons, G., & Solomons, H. Motor development in Yucatecan infants. *Developmental Medicine and Child Neurology,* 1975, **17,** 41–46.

Super, C. M. Patterns of infant care and motor development in Kenya. *Kenya Education Review,* 1976, in press.

Twitchell, T. E. Reflex mechanisms and the development of prehension. In K. J. Connolly (Ed.), *Mechanisms of motor skills development.* London: Academic Press, 1970. Pp. 25–45.

Wolff, P. Observation on newborn infants. *Psychosomatic Medicine,* 1959, **21,** 110–118.

Zelazo, P. Smiling to social stimuli: Eliciting and conditioning effects. *Developmental Psychology,* 1971, **4,** 32–42.

Zelazo, P. Smiling and vocalizing: A cognitive emphasis. *Merrill-Palmer Quarterly,* 1972, **18,** 349–365.

Zelazo, P., & Komer, M. Infant smiling to non-social stimuli and the recognition hypothesis. *Child Development,* 1971, **42,** 1327–1339.

Zelazo, P., Schwartz, G. E., & Kolb, S. Active exercise of the walking response in 2-, 6-, and 10-week-old infants. In preparation, 1976.

Zelazo, P., Zelazo, N., & Kolb, S. "Walking" in the newborn. *Science,* 1972, **177,** 1058–1059.

Comments on "From Reflexive to Instrumental Behavior"

Daniel G. Freedman

As I listened to Dr. Zelazo's presentation, I was immediately struck with its importance. Has anyone before demonstrated the continuity over the first year of a newborn reflex? Even if this is not a first, I am still amazed.

The fallout of this finding has hardly begun. Zelazo himself has some speculations, but I consider them rather weak. For example, he takes Super's remarks seriously and suggests that the advanced motor milestones seen in Kipsigis babies result from parental practice. However, it is well known by now that newborn and neonatal Black African infants of many different African tribes, as well as Afro-Americans, evidence motor precocity (Freedman, 1974; Leiderman, Babu, Dagia, Kraemer, & Leiderman, 1973; Warren, 1972) and it seems most likely that we are witnessing the results of differences in gene pools rather than in parental practices (Freedman, 1974). Additionally, among the Hausa of Nigeria, where I did some work, primary responsibility for rearing the youngest usually lies with an older sibling who for the most part carries the baby about on a sling; as far as I could observe, the babies there do not get special practice, yet motor precocity characterizes this group, too (Freedman, 1974).

Interestingly, Zelazo mentions that Yucatecan infants are also carried on a sling. However, here the fact of being carried about is used to explain late walking among this American Indian people. The gene-pool explanation seems applicable here, too, when one considers the data of Dennis (1940), who obtained the only other norms on walking among Indians. He found that the Hopi of Arizona also walked late (approximately 13 months) whether or not they were raised on a cradleboard. Our own data on the Navajo, now being gathered, indicate a similar lateness (when compared with Caucasian norms) and, as with Dennis' study, cradleboarding appears to make no difference.

All this sounds like a maturationist (sociobiologist?) reasserting his case, and that is of course a correct reading. In my opinion, the bulk of the evidence now available gives precious little reason to plan schedules for helping along normal growth patterns. Certainly there is ample evidence that practice and reinforcement make a difference, but perhaps working among the Indians of the Southwest chastens one's hubris, and engineering better humans—or even better sheep—seems a nasty thing even to contemplate. Any wise Navajo can tell you that Nature knows best, so let her be. Otherwise you may unloose more than you bargained for. I know that many of us in universities earn our keep by figuring out new ways to "therapize" and produce better humans, better crops and better sheep, so perhaps I had best end by wishing such efforts well. However, Mother Nature has been in the business of changing organisms a long time, and I should look to her for any real changes.

REFERENCES

Dennis, W. *The Hopi child.* New York: Appleton-Century, 1940.

Freedman, D. G. *Human infancy: An evolutionary perspective.* Lawrence Erlbaum Associates, 1974.

Leiderman, P. H., Babu, B., Dagia, J., Kraemer, C., & Leiderman, G. F. African infant precocity and some social influences in the first year. *Nature* (London), 1973, **242,** 247–249.

Warren, N. African infant precocity. *Psychological Bulletin,* 1972, **78,** 353–367.

A Reply to Freedman

Philip R. Zelazo

To propose that the stimulation of infant reflexes may illuminate development from reflexive to instrumental behavior is not to urge large-scale engineering of humans, sheep, or crops, as Freedman suggests. It is unnecessary to invoke the wisdom of the Navajo to prevent an all-out restructuring of man by curious and carefree academics. In fact, to suggest that maturation occurs without stimulation in nature is not only inaccurate but potentially hazardous advice, as the work of Dennis (1960) implies. The same wise Navajo who would advise us to leave nature alone would also assert that we existed in unity with nature, implying, among other things, that nature would provide the stimulation that allowed maturation to occur. We do not develop in a vacuum; we have air to breathe, water to drink, food to eat, land to walk on. There is no dispute that man is designed for this environment and that stimulation is inherent in existence (Scarr-Salapatek, this volume). The stimulation that we have used in our research is within the normal range of conditions encountered by man.

The Kipsigis and Desert San believe that some infant responses must be exercised, as Super (1976) and Konner (1973) have carefully documented with words, numbers, and photographs. Super has shown that the Kipsigis infants display relative precocity of precisely those responses that are stimulated—most notably sitting, standing, and walking. Relative precocity of individual responses does not occur simply by carrying these children around in a sling. Although genetic differences exist among infants, as Freedman demonstrates, it is not clear that African infant precocity is the result of differences in gene pools. Warren (1972) reviewed the existing research and found that most of the purported demonstrations of precocity had serious methodological shortcomings. He concluded that "African infant precocity cannot be taken as an acceptably established empirical phenomenon [p. 365]." Super attempted to meet some of Warren's objections by carefully and frequently testing his sample of Kipsigis babies, analyzing specific responses rather than summary scores, and documenting the child-rearing and socioeconomic correlates of precocity.

REFERENCES

Dennis, W. Causes of retardation among institutional children: Iran. *Journal of Genetic Psychology,* 1960, **96,** 47–59.

Konner, M. Newborn walking: Additional data. *Science,* 1973, **179,** 307.

Super, C. Patterns of infant care and motor development in Kenya. *Kenya Education Review,* 1976, in press.

Warren, N. African infant precocity. *Psychological Bulletin,* 1972, **78,** 352–367.

5

Developmental Psychobiology Comes of Age: A Discussion

Lewis P. Lipsitt

Brown University

The field of developmental psychology has strong roots in the science of biology. The Darwinian tradition, delivered to us through "the father of child psychology," G. Stanley Hall, urged that we heed the similarities between ontogenetic development, on one hand, and phylogenetic history, on the other. Our robust biological heritage comes from the extensive influence on our methodologies of developmental anthropometry, which was itself closely derived from embryology and anatomy. Developmental psychology has emerged from a felicitous coupling of two major characteristics of the biological science tradition: first, a striving for greater precision of measurement, and second, twentieth century man's intensive search for his place among species. These overriding concerns have led to the developmental psychologist's closer inquiry into how the child becomes man or woman.

Infants and children change with age. That is the first and least interesting law of human development. It is relatively uninteresting not only because it is obvious but because it is essentially descriptive and nonexplanatory. Nevertheless, the law has served the field well. It has yielded the developmental testing "movement," and it has impelled us to look more carefully for "the causes of behavioral change."

Developmental testing became early, and still remains, one of the major concerns of our field. Undeniably interesting issues have arisen in the context of psychometric work, such as whether developmental test performance in the first 18 months of life has anything to do with the proficiency of children on later intelligence tests or, more importantly, with the learning and performance capabilities of children in real-life pursuits.

Similarly, much energy and many pages of literature have been consumed in trying to settle such questions as whether there are real race differences in children's intelligence, whether early stimulation makes a difference in measured intelligence at later ages, and whether it can be determined how much of intelligent behavior is attributable to hereditary and congenital factors in contrast to experiential conditions.

The historical concern of the field of child development with the measured intelligence of children has, I think, tended to delay the full flowering of certain other empirical and theoretical concerns that are expected of a lively science. Specifically, the field has been, at least up to the past 10–20 years, more avid in its pursuit of descriptive laws of development than it has been in the study of specific processes and mechanisms of development. We were more concerned with what the organism was doing than why it did as it did. This is excusable, of course. Developmental psychology is a young science. It is in fact a young scientific conglomerate.

Scattered studies involving the experimental manipulative approach have appeared in the developmental literature throughout this century. Until recently, however, description rather than manipulation has been the methodology of choice. It is difficult to assess how the transition of our field into experimentalism really has taken place, and a retrospective accounting of the shift must inevitably slight someone's favorite rebel. A seminal article, which both heralded the shift and promoted it to an extent that its author probably could not have anticipated, was that by Kurt Lewin (1931) in his now classic application of the Galilean and Aristotelian dichotomy to the field of child development. Lewin's thesis, that developmental psychology had to move toward the discovery of causes of developmental change and away from the sheer descriptive assessment of infants and young children, was perhaps appreciated more fully at first by social psychologists than by developmental or child psychologists. Lewin and his colleagues and students carried out a number of investigations with children relating to motivation, group influences, and social preferences, such as the effects on children of autocratic, democratic, and laissez-faire permissions and pressures on their interpersonal behavior. It was not until about 20 years later, however, that studies of children emerged utilizing experimental manipulative techniques and sophisticated statistical procedures for the assessment of behavior change accruing as a function of cumulative experience.

The ascendancy in experimental psychology of a concern for learning processes was an important milestone. The attendant theoretical disputations occurring among the leaders, such as Hull, Tolman, and Guthrie, and later their successors, gave encouragement nonetheless to students of child behavior interested in the processes and mechanisms underlying experientially induced behavior change in children. Hull, in particular, encouraged his experimental psychology students to make their laboratory findings relevant or, at least, to seek parallels in everyday life of the behavioral laws investigated in the laboratory. The well-known applications to human behavior that have been drawn by such Hullian students as Miller, Mowrer, Dollard, Doob, and Sears need no further reference.

Robert Sears was especially interested in the effects of early experience on later behavior. He and his students generated numerous studies (Sears, Whiting, Nowlis, & Sears, 1953) seeking to establish the complex relationships between parental behavior and attitudes, on one hand, and children's aggressive and dependent behaviors, on the other. In this work, he drew on the assumption of cumulative effects of familial training on developmental outcome and, at the same time, sought to establish parallels between certain Freudian suppositions and those of learning theory, e.g., the understanding of children's displacement behavior in terms of the reinforcement history relating to past approach and avoidance responses.

It was inevitable thereafter that developmental psychology, most specifically that portion of it relating to learning processes and sensory reception, should become a laboratory science. Two articles that, as did Lewin's, both heralded and prompted the transition were by Spiker and McCandless (1954) and Stevenson (1955). The next two decades of experimental manipulative child psychology were devoted, first, to meticulous refinements of basic learning-process laws. Many of the elegantly designed and executed studies were, of course, replications and elaborations of studies previously carried out with animals. Such studies made theoretical and empirical contributions. Most of them produced a small increment in knowledge about the ways in which children's behavior was affected by variations, for example, in the number of trials administered, by stimulus similarity, by stress and anxiety factors, by the method of teaching a skill, or by the schedule of reinforcement under which learning occurred. Frequently, no variations in age of the child were of concern to the experimenter. No apologies are required, nor were many given, for the constricted age ranges investigated.

It was a period we had to go through, and it was one which clearly had a salubrious effect on our current position and legitimate outlook for the future.

These introductory remarks have been intended to convey that we can now go back to our original fundamental biological interest in development, with our identity problems for the most part behind us. We are now a sophisticated experimental science, with our roots firmly in the field of biology and with a primary commitment to observation and empirical documentation of basic mechanisms and processes. The selections prepared for this symposium show the great extent to which our reaffiliation with biology, and our newer view of ourselves as "developmental psychobiologists," guides our research endeavors.

I should not suppose that all of the contributors to this volume would characterize the recent history of our field in the same terms as I, nor should I think that each of them would be as happy as I about the tendency toward increased experimentalism. Indeed, the very nature of some studies, particularly those of a cross-cultural, anthropological sort such as Dan Freedman conducts, often prohibits the intrusion of experimental manipulative procedures and the assessment of "treatments." The culture is the independent variable, and the fascinating drawings that Freedman collects contain the dependent variables.

Freedman (Chapter 2) comes closer than any of the other contributors to traditional developmental psychology. The developmental traditionalist tested children of different ages, showing that behavior is different from one age step to another, and then postulated (with no other than circumstantial evidence) that later stages depended on prior stages for their character. Freedman tests multiple cultures under essentially comparable conditions and, noting the commonalities of similarly aged children across these cultures (in regard, for example, to the presence or absence of missiles in the drawings), concludes that children of the same age, regardless of culture, have similar fantasies or modes of creative expression. Of course, he goes one step further and, based on his world view and (again) circumstantial evidence, concludes that it is an inherently biological trait that male children tend to draw more vehicles and monsters than females, whereas females draw more flowers than males. Admittedly, one is struck by the "universality" of the phenomenon, in that the "law" seems to hold in all nine cultures for which Freedman has data. However, one must be struck also by the differences in proportions in the various cultures and, in some instances, by the reversals. For example, in Japanese children, the ratio of males to females for monster drawing was 57:12, whereas in a slightly different-aged population of Chinese children the comparable ratio was 10:4. Moreover, neither Ceylonese nor African children of either sex produced any monsters. Among Indian children, girls produced more monsters than boys by a ratio of approximately 12:5. Nonetheless, one is impressed. Flower drawing is more frequent in all nine cultures for females, except among the African children, where males and females do not differ in this and where few children draw flowers.

Freedman's position is an interactionist one despite the weight of the evidence he adduces on behalf of "universals" and in favor of race differences. Note the difference he finds between Chinese–American and European–American infants in their response on the Cambridge Neonatal Scales, for example. Newborn Caucasians more quickly and vigorously defended themselves when a cloth was placed for a few seconds over their faces. The Oriental children were impassive and exhibited very little motoric objection to such stimulation. It would be difficult to claim a "cultural-learning" basis for such differential responsivity in the first days of life. However, in the case of drawings of children from 5 to 7 years of age, there is no question about the opportunity for culture and family to have inculcated sex-role preferences, values, and fears. As a reasonable man, Freedman (Chapter 2) acknowledges ". . . the importance of social learning and societal input in the patterning of variation in male and female roles . . . [p. 53]" but he also insists on ". . . emphasizing that societal institutions do not arise, as it were, out of the blue [p. 53]." Continuing, he says: ". . . world-wide consistencies in institutionalized male–female roles appear to reflect phylogenetically adaptive differences in the sexes, differences that may already be seen in their incipient forms in very early infancy [p. 53]."

There is a big question and an empirical challenge here. We need to know more about the processes of socialization, more about the ways in which acculturation builds on hereditary or congenital givens. This requires, as a first step, the descriptions of early infant behavior under well-controlled testing conditions, which Freedman has given us, and then documentation of subsequent behavior. However, we need to know more than that. We need research designs that enable the documentation of how the later has grown out of the earlier. Why should or does society accommodate or acquiesce to apparently congenital sex differences by creating, if it does as Freedman suggests, an environment in which those congenital dispositions can thrive? It is not a foregone conclusion that this would be truly an adaptive or an adaptively constructive mode of societal response to sex differences. Society does not characteristically reinforce people who cry simply because they have happened to cry from the earliest moments in their lives.

Sandra Scarr-Salapatek's (Chapter 3) thoughtful and well-tempered statement on the relative contributions of genetic and experiential factors in infant development supports the theme just espoused. As she says: "Genetic effects on behavior are plausible only as the explanation incorporates biochemical pathways to morphological characteristics (e.g., brain structures) that mediate the gene–behavior links [p. 59]." She wants explanations cast in the form of mechanisms and processes (presumably antecedent–consequent relationships), which is likely to obviate studies seeking merely to lay a proportion of merit or blame on hereditary factors and another portion on experiential conditions. Explanations about the origins of intelligence must ultimately go beyond statistical reduction of the behavior into hereditary and environmental proportions of variance. As Anastasi (1958) has urged, the heredity versus environment question cannot be solved by asking how much, but only by asking how. In Scarr-Salapatek's terms: "Understanding sources of variation within a population or between populations is difficult enough, but accounting for human development per se is a far more difficult task [p. 61]."

Scarr-Salapatek's elaborations of Waddington's views (Chapter 3) on canalization in development does our field a service by calling attention once again to biological plasticity and behavioral adaptability. Waddington's thesis is that although everything is not possible developmentally, ". . . there are alternative developmental pathways [p. 64]." These pathways or "creods" are essentially open lines that can be selected and traversed. Once a line at a particular juncture is selected and entered, the other alternatives at that juncture are closed. It is rather like being an adoptable child in a social agency. Ten families known to the agency might be declared "suitable" for the adoption. One of the families gets the child, and the nine other possibilities are thereupon nullified. We can never know about the effects the other nine may have had on this child, for all of the effects henceforth must depend on the effects that the selected pathway (creod) has had on the child, through the imposition of constraints and provision of permissions. An interesting point which Scarr-Salapatek makes in this connection, and makes very well, is that many human behaviors are disposed toward canalization. For example, all cultures, one way or another and in due time, provide the setting or opportunity within which the child can try his or her feet at walking. It is seldom that society gives extra permission for walking before the age of 6 months and it must be unusual to find a culture or family that discourages or prohibits walking after 2 years of age. Therefore, walking behavior is exhibited not only because there is a basic biological competency for walking but because the human environment, perhaps also for biological reasons, provides the appropriate pathway for this disposition. It is important to appreciate in this connection that the universal permission afforded walking behavior by a certain age delimits the humane possibilities of studying the potential consequences of experiential deprivation in this domain. It is neither fatuous nor trite to suggest that human behavior is what it is because humans permit it to be so.

Among the permissions that parents (and later, culture and schools) may bestow on infants and children are numerous opportunities for providing experiences—experiences that in principle may facilitate learning, retard learning, induce or dispel fear, support identification and imitation, or support attachment and dependency or punish it. In short, children's caretakers have a wide berth. Although anthropologists show us how very different people are in some dimensions, it is also well to consider how similarly peoples round the world treat their infants and children. It is seldom that people, especially parents, deliberately treat children maliciously. Even in instances of child abuse, it is rare that the adult confesses to truly and persistently wanting to damage the child; instead, it is usually a matter of specific frustration or other situation-instigated aggressive act, at least in the case of child abuse in modern times. It is not the purpose to dwell here on the effects that may be imposed on children through specific abuses or general deprivation, but such real-life fortuitous "experiments" should not be overlooked as a valuable source of information about the developmental consequences of unfortunate and presumably deleterious child-rearing events.

The other side of the coin is easier to study. This is the question of whether "universal" behaviors, such as walking, talking, reading, and laughing, can be addressed experimentally with little or no threat of adverse reactions, either in the children studied or in the watchful public. It is not a foregone conclusion but an empirical matter that early practice in certain socially desirable behaviors has a beneficial effect on the child. The enterprise sufficiently lacks risk as to warrant judicious exploration.

Phil Zelazo (Chapter 4) has provided fascinating information on the possibility of facilitating walking behavior in infants by providing more than the usual opportunity for practice, which is generally considerable. The service that the Zelazo studies perform, however, goes beyond the mere demonstration that children can walk earlier than they usually do. He provides more than a mere demonstration that development is a matter of progressive appearances of programmed behaviors appearing right at the time when indeed they do show up. Walking is clearly a "biological" response in the sense of its universality, but it also has experiential precursors that depend on environmental permissions. I refer to leg exercise and subsequent opportunity for creeping, crawling, and pulling oneself to a standing position and opportunity to fall without occasioning so much punishment as to preclude or discourage further attempts to stand up. Zelazo's studies show that if the constraints are removed, or if the permissions are granted (depending on one's vantage point), walking can occur earlier than usual for that particular culture. Biological capacity is therefore experientially released. More important, however, is the demonstration that the early reflexive characteristics, i.e., the neurological repertoire with which the infant is endowed by species, are apparently intimately linked with the instrumental behaviors that the infant may later manifest.

This view of the developmental process whereby neural reflexes form the basis of later voluntary or operant action has not been articulated often, and there are precious few studies in which the supposition has been given a fair try. A biological sensitivity should encourage the view, and studies deriving from such a view, that the many reflexes of infancy must have some possible later function. The progression of reflexive behaviors needs to be studied from the beginning to full maturity. The term "maturity" in this instance, as opposed to its traditional use, refers as much to experiential expertise (i.e., peak performance under maximally facilitating environmental circumstances) as to "constitutional limits"—

which are in reality seldom tested in the presence of optimal experiential input.

The fascinating programmatic studies by Joseph Campos (Chapter 1), utilizing heart rate as a measure of emotional development in the infant, further support the implication of earlier remarks in this discussion that the manipulative approach of the experimental child psychologist must ultimately bring us back to a closer consideration of the biology of the developing individual. Campos has selected one particular psychobiological indicator as the dependent measure of emotional reactivity. His use of the single index of emotional reactivity has the capability of signaling perceptual reactions of the infant. If an infant shows a larger heart rate response on the deep side of a visual cliff than on the shallow side, therefore, this reveals the presence of a fear reaction but also informs us that the stimulus differences between deep and shallow have been perceived.

The heart rate response has a venerable history, and there is ample evidence that acceleration and deceleration represent disparate psychological reactions, defense in the first instance and orienting in the second. The response is therefore an excellent candidate for the study of "universal" psychobiological reactions and individual differences in them. Campos makes special capital of the bidirectional character of the heart rate response and, in an experiential *tour de force,* demonstrates a heart rate developmental shift with 5-month-old infants showing predominantly cardiac deceleration to the appearance of a stranger, whereas 9-monthers generally show accelerative responding, especially when the stranger is most intrusive. The heart rate response, then, is an environmental threat indicator. That such measures of heart rate coincide rather well with facial expressions in the older infant provides at once increased confidence in the "ethological validity" of the measure and a certain degree of security in the knowledge that heart rate measurement is somewhat more reliable than are judgments of physiognomic characteristics.

Although the study of autonomic nervous system indicators in the young child is still in its own infancy, the Campos experiments help pave the way for the study of simultaneously recorded electrophysiological responses of the infant in relatively natural life situations. It will become exceedingly important eventually to document the synchrony (and asynchrony where that is the case) of multiple responses in such situations as on the visual cliff or in the alternating company of familiar and strange persons. One should like to know especially about the manner in which the child's own operant behavior "drives" his autonomic responsivity, and vice versa. We need more information about the reciprocities between instrumental and autonomic responses, and about the ways in which the young child modulates specific aspects of its behavior on signal from some other response. We know that a newborn's sucking activity occurs in bursts, with the execution of a number of sucks apparently causing a temporary shutdown of sucking, whereupon the execution of a certain rest interval of no sucking signals the infant to begin a new sucking burst. In the same way, it is possible that, at some point, increased heart rate and other manifestations of fear in the presence of a stranger signals flight to the infant. This may "cause" the gaze to be averted in the precrawling child, or "cause" the crawling or walking child to retreat physically from the feared object or person.

RECIPROCATING AND INTERDEPENDENT RESPONSE PROCESSES IN NEONATAL SUCKING

The type of intraorganismic reciprocity of function to which I have just alluded is exemplified by some recent findings from my own research program. These relate to the effects on the newborn's sucking behavior and heart rate of changes in the tastants delivered into its mouth contingent on its own behavior. Although the sucking response of the newborn is an essentially elicited behavior, dependent on intraoral tactual stimulation, the infant's style of sucking is largely a matter of taste. Sucking behavior is modulated by the newborn to accord with the taste quality of the self-administered fluid. In the interface between the infant and the source of the tastant, i.e., the environment, it is truly difficult to designate which portions of the system are "stimulators" and which are "responders." It is actually a reciprocating system. Moreover, it depends heavily for its instigation, its continuation, and its rhythm on the hedonic receptivity of the persons entering the system.

In a study (Lipsitt, Reilly, Butcher, & Greenwood, in press) of 44 normal full-term newborns, 24 males and 20 females, testing was conducted on 2 consecutive days, using polygraph recording techniques. Mean age on initial testing (Day 1) was 54 hr (27–120 hr) and on Day 2, 78 hr (51–144 hr). All infants in this study, 33 bottle fed and 11 breast fed, were part of a longitudinal study; only some aspects of the newborn data are considered here.

Sucking behavior, heart rate, and respiration were recorded in each infant, five successive periods each of 2-min duration. Three of these were sucking for no fluid, followed by two periods of 15% sucrose sucking. About 35 sec intervened between periods, during which a computer printed out the interresponse time data (IRT) for the preceding period. The nipple was not removed between periods. The infant continued sucking under the same condition as in the preceding period. The beginning of a period following the 35-sec printout was initiated after the infant stopped sucking for at least 2 sec after the end of a burst.

At the end of the second sucrose period, the nipple was removed. There then ensued a 2-min period of polygraph recording during a "resting" state, defined as quiescent and with regular respiration, in which the infant neither sucked nor was stimulated in any way.

The results suggest a very interesting interplay between the sucking response and heart rate. They further substantiate a process that suggests a "savoring mechanism," which seems to be present already during the newborn period.

The computer printout at the end of each 2-min period provided a frequency distribution, for intersuck intervals under 2 sec, of sucking IRTs in 100-msec bins. The mean IRT could be calculated from the printout, using the midpoint of the bin as its numerical representation. Figure 5.1 is a polygraph record from this study, showing the final phase

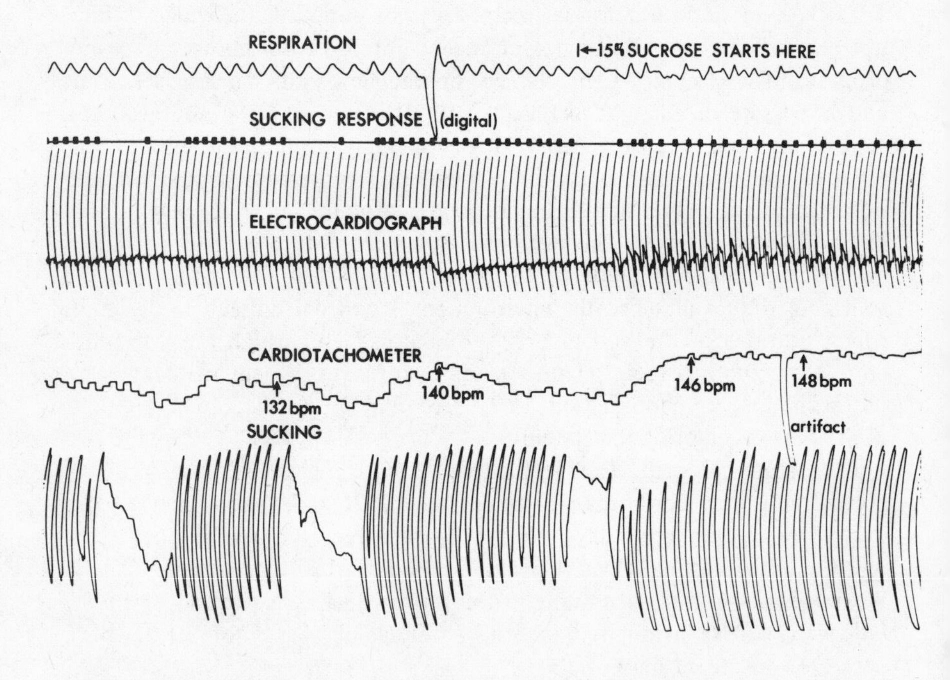

FIGURE 5.1 Exemplary polygraph record from 41-hr-old normal male, showing the last two bursts of no-fluid sucking preceding introduction of the sucrose sucking condition. The total polygraph record shown runs for 1 min. The top channel records respiration. The pen marker shows digital representation of criterion sucks, which receive .02-ml drops of fluid during sucrose period. The next operating channel is the electrocardiograph (EKG), below which is the cardiotachometer transformation of the interbeat intervals. The bottom channel is the sucking record. Long sucking bursts are characteristic of sucrose sucking. Heart rate during sucrose may be seen to rise to a higher level (and remain there) than during no-fluid sucking.

of nonnutritive (no-fluid) sucking in comparison with the first phase of sucrose sucking for an exemplary subject of this experiment. The figure demonstrates the manner, described quantitatively in the next two paragraphs, in which the switch from no-fluid sucking to sucrose sucking produces a very rapid alteration in sucking style, leading to longer IRTs under the sucrose condition as well as shorter and fewer rest periods (or interburst intervals). Moreover, even in the presence of slower-rate sucking, the heart rate is higher during sucrose sucking, as can be seen in the more densely packed beats in the EKG channel or in the heightened cardiotachometer recording. The higher heart rate during sucrose sucking suggests the operation of a hedonic mechanism whereby the newborn slows its sucking behavior, perhaps thus stimulating a greater receptive area of the tongue with the fluid, and simultaneously signals with a higher heart rate its enhanced "joy" with the stimulus. The observed effect takes place in this procedure with as small an amount of fluid per suck, as in this study, as .02 ml.

Table 5.1 shows the five sucking parameters under the no-fluid and sucrose sucking conditions. The mean and modal IRTs are greater when

TABLE 5.1
Comparison of the Means (2-min units) of Five Suckling Parameters under No-Fluid and Sucrose Sucking Conditions over a 2-day Period[a]

	Day 1		Day 2		Day 1/Day 2	
	Mean	SD	Mean	SD	r	p^r
No-fluid sucking (N = 41)						
Total responses	88.3	23.2	96.6	30.9	.62	.001
IRTs > 2 min (rests)	8.1	2.6	8.7	2.8	.65	.001
Responses/burst	12.9	15.5	11.2	6.1	.79	.001
Mode IRT	620.3	99.0	572.8	61.9	.37	.05
Mean IRT	657.8	81.7	611.9	56.0	.42	.01
15% Sucrose sucking (N = 40)						
Total responses	103.0	28.2	106.2	27.6	.08	–
IRTs > 2 min (rests)	5.3	2.7	5.9	3.5	.13	–
Responses/burst	29.7	34.2	24.2	21.7	.03	–
Mode IRT	838.1	109.9	771.3	115.7	.63	.001
Mean IRT	855.8	105.3	786.9	85.8	.71	.001

[a] From the initial group of 44 subjects, three failed to suck nonnutritively on Day 1, thus reducing the analyzable records to 41 for both days. In all, four subjects had nonanalyzable sucrose sucking records, two on Day 1 (these overlapping with the no-fluid failures), reducing the sucrose subjects to 40. The measures are based upon 2-min means, three for the no-fluid and two for the sucrose condition.

TABLE 5.2
Heart Rate (beats/min) during Resting and When Sucking for No Fluid or Sucrose, and Correlation Coefficients (r) Comparing Day 1 and Day 2[a]

		Day 1		Day 2		Combined		Day 1/Day 2	
	N	Mean	SD	Mean	SD	Mean	SD	*r*	p^r
Basal	44	113.8	16.7	118.7	18.1	116.3	14.2	.29	<.05
No-fluid sucking	40	124.0	14.5	123.4	13.6	123.8	12.2	.46	<.01
Sucrose sucking	39	145.7	15.5	147.4	12.3	146.6	13.1	.71	<.001

[a] Failures to suck account for reductions of *N* from the initial group of 44, except in one case in which the heart rate record during sucking was unreadable.

sucking is for sucrose than when sucking under a no-fluid condition, and the number of responses per burst is twice as large. Also, more rest periods (IRTs less than 2 sec) occur under the no-fluid condition. Consequently, despite the faster rate of sucking within bursts under the no-fluid condition, more sucks per minute are emitted under sucrose. All these effects are reliable.

Table 5.2 compares the heart rate of infants during sucking periods with basal heart rate without the nipple. Very interestingly, the mean heart rate under no-fluid sucking was significantly higher than the basal rate. In turn the mean heart rate under sucrose sucking was higher than under the no-fluid condition. Although sucking rate within bursts is reduced when the infant sucks for sucrose, heart rate nevertheless increases reliably.

Recent studies completed in this laboratory indicate that changes from less sweet to sweeter fluids produce orderly changes in these response parameters in the directions just shown, and that the phenomenon is not limited to comparisons of no-fluid with fluid sucking conditions (Crook & Lipsitt, in press).

The more we study the human neonate under rather precise response-measurement conditions afforded by the polygraph and associated apparatus, such as the computer, the more are we impressed, first, by the fine interplay between the various congenital responses of the newborn and, second, by the extent to which the newborn's behavior and psychophysiological indices are affected by the environmental resources available to the infant at any given moment. For example, the manual introduction of 10% sucrose into the infant's mouth in the presence of a refusal to suck almost immediately generates sucking behavior that persists even on the subsequent withdrawal of that sucrose incentive. Similarly, experience in sucking for a sweet substance for a 5-min period affects the infant's subsequent behavior, at least for the next 5 min, when offered a less sweet incentive (Kobre & Lipsitt, 1972).

An important feature of our experimental techniques is that the infant is studied not just in the presence of stimulating features of the environment, which have been under the control of the experimenter, but also under conditions in which the infant is offered the opportunity to self-regulate. That is, our incentive conditions were such that we simply made available to the infant innocuous but variable reinforcing conditions, to which we studied the infant's response. The newborn through its instrumental or operant activity "engaged the system." I think that we are progressing toward a model for the interaction between an infant and its environment that acknowledges the considerable role that the infant's own congenital response propensities play, including those that are hedonically controlled or are activated by reinforcement-seeking mechanisms. Involved is not merely a stimulus–response relationship in which the environment or the infant's caretaker serves as stimulus and the subject responds, or even one in which the infant serves as stimulus and the environment responds. Instead, it is one in which there is constant reciprocity between the organism and environment, between the infant and the caretaker, in which each serves as stimulus and each responds. Both operate, at least in part, according to incentive principles which can and will be discovered. This too simple view of human nature and human development must yield to more complex models as we learn more, but we can learn more only by starting at the beginning.

SUCKLING AND RESPIRATORY OCCLUSION

The idea of behavioral reciprocity is, as stated, not limited to the communication of one psychobiological system of the infant with another of its systems. It also involves reciprocating relationships between the infant and the other persons in its life. The mother–infant interaction especially is a two-way affair, and this entire subject of reciprocating relationships is one deserving of much greater attention than it has received. The English pediatrician Mavis Gunther (1955, 1961) made some close observations of the fascinating ways in which the nursing mother and her infant affected each other reciprocally, immediately after birth, and quite possibly with lasting effects. The nursing couplet is comprised of a pair of persons that happen to be, or so it seems, excellent operant conditioners of one another. Gunther has described the situation in which the nursing newborn oftens finds itself. When the newborn is suckling at the breast, its nostrils periodically and fortuitously become occluded. This results in an aversive reaction on the part of the infant, involving various manifestations of withdrawal from the nipple and breast. The newborn ordinarily sucks with a secure pressure seal between its lips and the nipple. Unlatching from the breast once on it is not accomplished easily, particularly with a hungry infant. When threatened with nasal occlusion, therefore, the baby first engages in minor head movements, swaying the head from side to side and pulling its head backwards. Sometimes these actions succeed in freeing the nasal passages for breathing. If these maneuvers do not succeed, however, the normal infant executes a more vigorous pattern of behavior, such as arm waving and pushing against the mother's breast, this being often accompanied by facial vasodilation. Ultimately, if none of these maneuvers succeeds in wresting the infant free of the offending object, crying occurs. Under such circumstances, the baby is reinforced for retreating from the breast rather than remaining at it. Gunther described some observed instances in which the infant was noted to show reluctance when put to the breast after such an apparently aversive experience. Although Gunther does not phrase the sequence of activities as such, the stimulating event, the resulting reaction, and the subsequent aversion to the feeding situation may be easily conceptualized as one of operant learning.

Having observed such a sequence of events on a number of occasions, and being interested in the possible predictive significance of neonatal reflexes and their elicited vigor, I have been prompted to speculate on the possible psychological significance of early aversive behaviors and the role that these may play in the early reciprocating relationship between the newborn and its mother. The following remarks relate to the possible significance of the neonatal respiratory occlusion reflex, the same pattern of response that Dr. Freedman has tested in Oriental and Caucasian infants.

ANGRY BEHAVIOR IN THE NEWBORN, AND THE ONTOGENY OF AGGRESSION

Aversive behavior occurs in human infants under conditions in which biological threat exists. In its milder forms, such behavior is manifested in autonomic and withdrawal responses to intense stimulation, such as bright lights, noxious tactile stimuli, unpleasant odorants and tastes, trigeminal stimulants, and loud noises. The amount of active response occurring to such stimulation is directly proportional to stimulus intensity, with very intense stimulation culminating in crying.

Angry behavior may be defined in terms of the presence and vigor of autonomic and withdrawal response to noxious stimulation. Aggressive behavior, in contrast, may be taken to refer to responses of the baby, in the presence of anger, that have the function of thwarting perpetuation of the instigating noxious stimulation. In ordinary feeding circumstances, such defensive behavior can be fortuitously directed against the mother. Stimulation that supports or threatens respiratory occlusion tends to elicit a response pattern consisting of five components, which may be viewed as a fixed action pattern beginning with mild responsivity and proceeding toward extreme arousal if the stimulus condition is not removed. The five steps involved, as noted earlier, are (1) side to side head waving; (2) head withdrawal, with backward jerks and grimacing; (3) facial vasodilation; (4) arm jabbing; and (5) crying. The continuum of response is here defined as angry behavior, which can be seen to abate when the threatening or noxious stimulation is reduced.

Such behavior often occurs in the natural course of infant feeding. When anger is elicited in the newborn to respiratory occlusion, the action pattern has the effect of freeing the respiratory passages, by displacing the offending object or by impelling the mother to adjust her feeding position. The freeing from occlusion constitutes a reinforcement condition that can increase the probability of its occurrence under this and similar future conditions. The anger response may occur subsequently with a shorter latency, or even anticipatorily to less intense but similar stimulating conditions. Still late in ontogeny, it may occur without direct (exteroceptive) instigation at all. Moreover, such "aggressive" behavior may be mediated by anger generated from circumstances entirely different from those in which the behavior has been first learned. The learning mechanisms involved in the acquisition of aggressive behavior are those presumed implicated in other forms of instrumental learning. Initially, a congenital response pattern (anger) is elicited by experiential circumstances conducive to its expression. Components of that action pattern are selectively reinforced, following which these behaviors (now called aggressive) are learned and perpetuated through periodic practice, with reinforcement renewed on subsequent occasions.

This conceptualization has implications for the developmental elucidation of love as well as aggression. In this view, concepts of drive states or instincts relating to aggression and affection are gratuitous. Aggression and love may be considered as requiring "objects" toward which behavior is directed. Newborn emotional behavior is undirected at first; the persons available during the episodes of negative and positive emotional arousal, however, become the recipients of aggression and affection through learned association supported by systematic reinforcement. Individual differences in the experiential requirements for eliciting early emotional responsivity, including anger, must be pertinent to the course and strength of acquired aggressive and affectionate behavior patterns.

The foregoing comments are, as must be appreciated, entirely speculative and theoretical, except for their evidential basis in the observations of Gunther and others who have documented the infantile response to brief respiratory occlusion in the natural feeding situation. The thesis relating this type of behavior to the possible development of aggression is presented as a heuristic model of reciprocating relationships (Lipsitt, 1973; Newson, 1974) between mother and infant as well as for the "content," the verification of which is largely wanting. The following elaborations are presented in the same spirit.[1]

THE NEWBORN AS A HEDONIC RESPONDER

Newborns engage in systematic, replicable, congenital patterns of behavior from the earliest moments after birth. These behavior patterns engage immediately in a reciprocating relationship with the environment. The moment a baby is born, stimuli impinge on its receptors, producing changes in the infant's behavior that in turn alter the effective stimulation from the environment. Experience has an immediate effect on the baby, and the baby immediately alters the world in which it lives.

The newborn has in its behavioral repertoire an important tendency to regret and divert threats to its biological safety. Numerous aversive responses can be observed to noxious stimulation. A sudden increase in illumination occurring in the vicinity of the infant's open eyes, for example, causes the lids to close. If the skin surface is touched with great pressure or is pricked by a pointed object, the infant withdraws the offended part of its anatomy from the stimulus. If a noxious trigeminal stimulant is presented, the baby turns its head from the locus of stimulation and shows by facial expression and vocalization that the experience is disturbing. On stimulation with bitter quinine, withdrawal of the tongue occurs. Each of the sensory modalities of the newborn can be excessively stimulated to produce its own aversive style of response, always culminating in crying when lesser manifestations of aversion fail to enable escape.

Although much is known about the newborn's appetitive and generally pleasurable responsivity, little attention has been paid to the other side of the coin. One particular type of threat that occurs to the newborn, even under the most favorable of rearing circumstances, can be observed under

[1] Many of the ideas contained here concerning the possible emotional significance of the respiratory occlusion response of newborns as well as "failure to thrive" and "crib death" were presented (Lipsitt, 1971) in a colloquium talk at the University of California at Los Angeles Medical School, Department of Psychiatry, as part of a series on the development of aggression. The research cited here was supported by grants from the USPHS (HD 03911) and The Grant Foundation.

controlled conditions without placing the infant in developmental jeopardy. This is the momentary respiratory occlusion that frequently occurs when the infant is in the arms of its mother, at the breast. It is possible that this type of stimulation is actually necessary for favorable development. A test of this response appears as an item on the Graham (1956) scale of neonatal response. A test item like it is also included in the Brazelton (1973) Scale, called the Defensive Reaction.

It is not necessary for actual respiratory occlusion to be administered to elicit the behavior typical of the infant's "respiratory occlusion pattern." If a relatively flat object or gauze pad is put over the newborn's mouth and nostril area, even without actually occluding the respiratory passages, an aversive response occurs, with great variations in latency and vigor from one infant to another. The five-stage pattern of behavior described previously is typical. Although the sequence of these actions is seemingly fixed and is uniform across normal children, infants vary considerably in the rapidity with which they first respond (as reported by Daniel Freedman), the amount of time they take in executing the five stages, and the vigor with which they "engage." In the most lusty infants, great energy is mobilized to avert the offensive condition.

I am not prepared to say that this early manifestation of self-protection is intentional in the usual sense. All observers of the behavior are struck, however, with the functional utility of the response pattern. The response, is, in fact, a lifesaver. This can be best appreciated when the infant is observed lying prone in a crib. If the head is turned to the midline position, with the mouth and nostrils buried momentarily in the mattress, the infant lifts its head very quickly and turns to the preferred, tonic-neck-reflex position. It may well be that practice of the response in the earliest weeks of life is essential.

Casual observations of infants in their cribs suggest that practice in retrieving themselves from respiratory occlusion is virtually inevitable. It is possible to draw on Dr. Zelazo's thinking and data here in supposing that for respiratory retrieval from threat to occur properly at around 2 or 3 months of age, prior practice of the response must have occurred to bring the infant to a level of skill in executing it whereby it can occur, even while the infant sleeps, under urgent conditions of threat. It is known that myelinization occurs at a rapid rate within the first few months of life. It is known also that many of the congenital responses observable in newborns, such as the grasp reflex, the Babkin, the Babinski, and other neural responses, diminish in elicitability and intensity by about 3 months of age, to be superseded by voluntary instrumental behaviors. The grasp reflex, for example, which is initially elicited simply through tactile stimulation on the palms of the infant's hands, is engaged in voluntarily and in the service of grasping by 3 months of age. Following Dr. Zelazo here, it may be that deprivation of grasping experience within the first 3 months of life leads to a deficit in grasping skill in later months .

RELEVANCE OF DEVELOPMENTAL PSYCHOBIOLOGY TO CRIB DEATH

The absence of or deficiency in the respiratory occlusion response may be related to the occurrence of the still unexplained, so-called "crib death" that takes the lives of a large number of infants at around 2 and 3 months of age. Many infants who succumb as "crib death" cases are known to have had a mild cold, usually described as "sniffles," just prior to their unfortunate death. Still others have been diagnosed on autopsy as having pneumonitis, presumably not so serious as to cause death. It is an empirical problem for developmental psychologists and psychobiologists to determine whether respiratory occlusion, and the failure to make appropriate adjustive responses to such occlusion, are pertinent factors in such deaths. Throat-clearing responses in the older child and adult are so prevalent and facile that, as with so many mature and fairly universal behaviors, we do not concern ourselves much with their ontogeny. It is possible, however, that just as learning (and failure to learn) are important antecedents of life-saving responses (and their absence) in other spheres of human activity, so also is the learning of maneuvers to prevent respiratory occlusion necessary for the survival of the infant.

It is not inconceivable that a modicum of early practice is required for the infant to achieve a suitable level of "respiratory retrieval" when faced with the threat of occlusion. The infants who achieve the required minimum of practice are perhaps those whose experience at retrieval has been most frequent and most vigorous. These would be the infants who at birth and shortly thereafter have vigorous responses to the threat of a respiratory occluding stimulus. That is to say, most practice in this situation is probably self-administered, as the baby lies in his crib, especially in the prone position, and as the infant moves around among blankets, hands, and other objects that are so readily brought to the mouth by the infant's own arms. In this connection, one wonders whether the lethargy of response displayed by the "failure-to-thrive infant" may not have had its earliest representation in a deficiency of this and similar neonatal response patterns, or in the failure of opportunity to practice early congenital patterns of behavior.

REFERENCES

Anastasi, A. Heredity, environment, and the question "How?" *Psychological Review,* 1958, **65,** 197–208.

Brazelton, T. B. *Neonatal behavioral assessment scale.* (National Spastics Society Monographs) London, William Heinemann Medical Books Ltd., 1973.

Crook, C. K., & Lipsitt, L. P. Neonatal nutritive sucking: Effects of taste stimulation upon sucking rhythm and heart rate. *Child Development,* 1976, in press.

Graham, F. K. Behavioral differences between normal and traumatized newborns: 1. The test procedures. *Psychological Monographs,* 1956, No. 427, 70.

Gunther, M. Instinct and the nursing couple. *Lancet,* 1955, **1,** 575.

Gunther, M. Infant behavior at the breast. In B. Foss (Ed.), *Determinants of infant behavior.* London: Methuen, 1961. Pp. 37–44.

Kobre, K. R., & Lipsitt, L. P. A negative contrast effect in newborns. *Journal of Experimental Child Psychology,* 1972, **14,** 81–91.

Lewin, K. The conflict between Aristotelian and Galilean modes of thought in contemporary psychology. *Journal of General Psychology,* 1931, **5,** 141–162.

Lipsitt, L. P. Infant anger: Toward an understanding of the ontogenesis of human aggression. Unpublished paper presented at the Department of Psychiatry, The Center for the Health Sciences, University of California at Los Angeles, March 4, 1971.

Lipsitt, L. P. Reciprocating relationships in infant behaviour: Congenital and experiential determinants. *Bulletin of the British Psychological Society,* 1973, **26,** 56 (Abstract).

Lipsitt, L. P., Reilly, B. M., Butcher, M. J., & Greenwood, M. M. The stability and interrelationships of newborn sucking and heart rate. *Developmental Psychobiology,* 1976, in press.

Newson, J. Towards a theory of infant understanding. *Bulletin of the British Psychological Society,* 1974, **27,** 251–257.

Sears, R. R., Whiting, J. W. M., Nowlis, V., & Sears, P. S. Some child-rearing antecedents of aggression and dependency in young children. *Genetic Psychology Monographs,* 1953, **47,** 135–236.

Spiker, C. C., & McCandless, B. R. The concept of intelligence and the philosophy of science. *Psychological Review,* 1954, **61,** 255–266.

Stevenson, H. W. The experimental studies of children's learning. *Journal of Genetic Psychology,* 1955, **87,** 323–330.

6

Three Themes in Develomental Psychobiology

Jerome Kagan

Harvard University

The eras of an intellectual discipline are delineated by sets of central questions, each yoked to preferred methods of inquiry. Some questions are answered, if only temporarily; many are discarded because they were improperly framed; most are reworded to accommodate to new information. Physicists know why eclipses occur, do not worry about the "aether," and attempt to determine the number of basic particles rather than define an atom.

Psychologists too, have answered, discarded, or rephrased questions during the short history of the discipline. We now have some insight into the nature of color vision, do not ask about the essence of will, and probe the conditions that monitor the performance of a coherent set of actions rather than seek the intrinsic meaning of reinforcement. Developmental psychologists, in a field with an even shorter history, have clarified some puzzles that provoked brooding among sixteenth century scholars. Infants apparently see hues as adults (Bornstein, 1975) and are afraid of events they do not understand (Kagan, 1976). We have stopped looking for the spirits that bewitch infants, and have begun to substitute statements about the developmental course of specific competences in task contexts for principles about intelligence.

One of the most vital changes in perspective regards the role of experience. We used to ask, "How does experience alter the child's behavior?" because we assumed that all experience had some effect on the young child. We now entertain the possibility that maturational constraints render some experiences irrelevant, for the effect of experience is dependent in part on its timing. Hence, we wish to know how the developing brain uses varied experience to permit change. Developmental psychologists generally wish to understand four quite different classes of phenomena:

1. We want to explain normative ontogenetic changes in those behaviors and competences that appear to be universal and appreciate that the interaction of maturational and environmental events is necessary to account for the fundamental phenomena.
2. We wish to explain interindividual variation in behavior in specific contexts during a particular developmental stage. Some children do not show object permanence until 1 year; others display this ability at 7 months.
3. We wish to explain intraindividual variation in different contexts during the same era; a child is likely to smile at a mask of a human face at 5 months of age, but not to a car rolling down a ramp. At 30 months the probability of smiling to these two events is completely reversed.
4. Finally, we wish to explain extreme deviance, phenomena like schizophrenia, suicide, and autism, which, like freak waves on an ocean's surface, are unusually difficult to predict.

The elegant essays in this volume, which are essentially concerned with the first two enigmas, address the two major themata in contemporary developmental psychology—the interaction of biological and psychological factors, and the validity and meaning of stages in development. But there is one obvious lacuna. These contributions fail to deal with the relevance of context. This brief epilogue is addressed to these three themes.

THE RELATION BETWEEN BIOLOGICAL MATURATION AND PSYCHOLOGICAL EXPERIENCE

The lawful changes that occur over the human lifespan are obviously under the guidance of the rather strict script contained in the genome, which guarantees that we will crawl before we run and mimic before we speak. All 2-year-olds carry a small number of potentialities, which attract them to contour and curvilinearity and dispose them to stop playing when a stranger enters the room. Ernst Mayr (1974) has called these *closed systems*. The *open systems* are created by the experiential events that control the variability and the time of appearance of inherited competences, as well as the intensity, frequency, and asymptotic level of functioning of these dispositions. These open systems define the profile of psychological characteristics that allow us to detect class, regional, ethnic, and national differences with greater ease than is good for us or for society. The complementary action of closed and open systems is a new way of phrasing the sentence, which appears in a similar form in almost every textbook on human behavior: The interactions between biological and environmental forces determine the psychological growth of the organism. What does that 14-word sentence mean?

Our inability to answer that question and invent a crisp metaphor for the textbook phrase is multidetermined. One reason derives from the historical debate between science and the church that began almost five centuries ago. The accommodation of each institution to the other led to a treaty that "awarded" material events to science and psychic ones to the church. Each institution was supposed to honor the intellectual sovereignity of the other. The major philosophical statements written in the seventeenth and eighteenth centuries were attempts to keep this truce sturdy as the assumptions of science became more appealing than those of the church. There is a second reason—less profound but of consequence. Analysis, which is the preferred strategy of science, assumes a special form in psychology. Since psychological phenomena are so variable, social scientists were drawn to statistical techniques that were based on the presupposition that one could analyze a unitary phenomenon—say a child's height, achievement score in reading, or hallucinations—into separate biological and experimental causes and assign a weight to each. We resist Whitehead's metaphysics, which assumes that the raw materials of science are occasions of experience, each with a duration and an essential unity:

> Any attempt to analyze it into component parts injures it in some way. But we cannot do anything with it unless we do analyze it. A first step toward analysis is to dissect the unity into an experiencing subject and an experienced object. The dividing line between these two is both arbitrary and artificial. It can be drawn through various positions and wherever it is drawn it is never anything more than a convenience [Waddington, 1975, p. 4].

A favorite model of analysis is the multiple-regression equation, whose partial coefficients imply that some factors are more important than others. This conceptualization of nature often prevents us from viewing an event as the product of a coherence of forces. Consider a Christmas snowfall created by the complementary interaction of humidity and temperature. It seems inappropriate to ask which factor is more critical, or to assign different beta weights to temperature and humidity. We seem to have less trouble acknowledging such complementary interactions when both forces are in a material mode than when the names for the forces originate in different metalinguistic domains, such as biology and psychology.

The power of analysis in biological research has persuaded many of the utility of treating discrete, material neurological elements as primary and the less discrete psychological events as part of the former. But consider the case of a Taiwanese merchant who visits a shaman because of a chronic pain in his chest. The local shaman tells the merchant that he has angered an ancestor, and if he makes restitution, he will be relieved. He leaves the shaman with less distress than when he arrived (Kleinman, 1975).

Many Western physicians and psychologists are likely to spend hours arguing whether the symptom resulted primarily from psychological or physiological factors. But suppose there is a synergy between the merchant's physiology and his psychology. Many Taiwanese with a similar physiology but fewer worries might not develop the same somatic symptoms; many with a similar collection of uncertainties but not the same physiology would not have the distress. An infant with brain stem damage resulting from perinatal anoxia who is raised in a familial environment in which little psychological acceleration occurs will display cognitive deficits at age 6. A child with the same set of birth conditions growing up in an environment that provides many opportunities for cognitive development will not display the intellectual deficit (Broman, Nichols, & Kennedy, 1975). A black child in an all white classroom produces a certain quality of psychological tension; the same child in a black classroom does not. Each of these examples, and we could offer many more, illustrates a more general principle, namely, mutual interaction between an element and the larger field in which it exists creates a new entity. The new entity is not a part of either the element or the field, and the sentences that describe the transcendental entity cannot be completely replaced with sentences that describe the original element and field without losing some meaning. A hallucination is a part of neither the brain nor the structures created by past history. The field of physics provides the best metaphor. An electric charge in an electromagnetic field mutually influence each other. The charge is described in terms of velocity and energy, the field is described in terms of strength, and their interaction produces a third, quite different phenomenon—radiation—which is described in terms of frequency. The radiation is neither part of the field nor part of the charge; it is a product of the interaction of charge and field.

Mental phenomena (for example, the perception of red, the ability to recall five numbers, or smiling to a face) are analogous to radiation, for they result from the mutual interaction of neural structures and psychological processes in the larger field we call the central nervous system. The perception of red is no more a part of the cells of the central nervous system than radiation is part of the field or the electric charge that generated it. Biological forces contribute to and are necessary for psychological phenomena, but the characteristics of the latter are, like radiation, a product of the interaction. The most detailed knowledge of neural organization, including all the significant synapses in a chicken embryo at a given stage of embryogenesis, would not permit prediction of the actual movements of the embryo at that stage. All we can say is that the state of differentiation of the nervous system at a given stage limits the range of behavioral potentialities. The maturation of the nervous system sets both constraints and permissiveness on the range of behaviors possible, but cannot explain them.

Consider the universal developmental phenomenon of "separation anxiety." The infant must be at a particular stage of cognitive maturation in order to protest his caretaker's departure (Kagan, 1976) for such distress rarely occurs before 8 months of age. During the period from 8 to 24 months, when protest is most likely to occur, the enormous variation in the frequency and intensity of the protest that follows maternal departure is likely to be a function of the interaction of experience and the child's temperament. Firstborn 1-year-olds living in an infant house on an Israeli kibbutz protest separation with greater intensity than laterborns; Bushmen children living on the Kalahari Desert are more likely to display separation distress than American children during the normal period of its display.

A second illustration of this idea comes from our recent longitudinal study of Chinese and Caucasian children, some of whom were being reared totally at home, some of whom were attending a day care center. The children were observed in a pair of play sessions at 13, 20, and 29 months. Initially they played with an interesting set of toys while their mother read a magazine. After almost a half hour of play, an unfamiliar child of the same sex, and ethnicity, and that child's mother were introduced into the room. Changes in duration of playing, vocalization, and proximity to the mother were coded as indexes of the child's degree of apprehension to the unfamiliar peer. Chinese and Caucasian home-reared children showed an inverted U-shaped function for inhibition of play with a peak inhibition at 20 months (Kagan, 1976). That is, there was a greater decrease in time playing, comparing solo with peer session, at 20 months than at 13 or 29 months for both ethnic groups. However, the degree of apprehension, as indexed by proximity to mother, inhibition of vocalization, and inhibition of play, was significantly greater for the Chinese than for the Caucasian children.

Biological changes in the central nervous system, interacting with the experiences that characterize the larger field, lead most children to display maximal apprehension to an unfamiliar peer somewhere in the middle of the second year. Processes probably related to the temperament of the Chinese child and special experiences in the home contribute to a greater level of apprehension. This finding suggests that one must distinguish between growth functions for phenomena dictated by a maturational script and individual variation, within a particular developmental era, in the level or qualtiy of the behavioral phenomenon. We suggest that it is not always useful to assign different beta weights to the genetic forces that direct the maturational events or temperamental dispositions and to the experiential field in which these forces operate. We can and must discover the functional relations among these forces, as physicists have discovered the functional relationships among charge, field, and radiation.

THE MEANING OF STAGE

Although psychological change seems at the surface to be continuous, some psychologists believe that it is theoretically useful to organize these changes into stages. The word stage has two meanings—one descriptive and the other theoretical. The former, which is relatively easy to understand, refers to a correlation among clusters of psychological characteristics during particular periods in development. Embryologists distinguish between the stage of the embryo and that of the fetus, the latter being characterized by growth and enlargement of organs rather than differentiation. At a descriptive level that distinction seems reasonable and even helpful, but it does not explain anything about growth. It is a little like saying that an automobile journey from Boston to New York consists of two stages—one prior to the Merritt Parkway where traffic is light, and one from the Merritt Parkway to Manhattan where traffic is heavy.

Most psychologists are dissatisfied with a descriptive concept of stage and want a theoretical construct that states something about the necessary relations between the structures and processes of successive eras.

Campos' imporant contribution to this volume implies the emergence of a stage toward the end of the first year. Campos reports cardiac acceleration to the visual cliff among 9-month-olds but deceleration at 5 months of age. This difference in the direction of heart rate to the deep side of the cliff before and after 9 months of age is one example from a very large set of behavioral changes that appear between 7 and 13 months. For example, there is a dramatic increase in attention to transformations of familiarized auditory and visual events between 7 and 9 months of age in both American and Guatemalan children. There is also an increase in inhibition in the reaching for novel objects, and the emergence of stranger and separation anxiety. Should these changes be viewed as the product of a new common structure or a new process? A clue to the answer comes from the fact that there is a major increase in the ability to retrieve information from memory somewhere around 8 to 10 months of age. For example, 8-month-old children in the "*A* not *B*" object permanence paradigm will not perform correctly when the delay between hiding the object in the new place and allowing the child to reach is long, say 7 sec, but will perform correctly if the delay is short, for example, 1–3 sec. Delayed-response performance tests on monkeys also point to the growth of memory processes in the middle of the first year (see Rosenblum & Alpert, 1974).

It is likely that the changes that occur between 8 and 13 months result in large measure from an increase in the ability to retrieve structures from memory that represent events and objects that are not in the immediate field. The 9-month-old, but not the 6-month-old, is able to retrieve (not just recognize) schemata for events not in his or her present field that happened more than a few seconds earlier. Schaffer has also suggested that the ability to activate from memory schemata for absent objects and to use them to evaluate a situation are critical for the changes that occur at this time (Schaffer, 1974). We are suggesting that the stage we call "short-term memory" collapses soon after every experience in the child under 8 months. But after that time changes in the central nervous system allow the infant to retrieve information transduced earlier. The data imply that the essence of the performance we call the "object concept" is not the acquisition of a new structure (the belief that objects are permanent) but rather the emergence of a new cognitive competence.

The movement called "developmental psychobiology" recognizes the temporary usefulness of psychological stages that are monitored by a child's changing biology, for the psychological functioning of a 4-year-old is obviously different from that of a 1-year-old. But it is less obvious that the additional assumption of a thick cord of connection between stages, a contingent relation between earlier and later structures, is as useful. This idea is attractive to the Western mind because of a predilection toward the notion of unitary deep structures that explain phenotypically diverse performances. It is less pleasing to consider successive classes of behavior, each resting on its own base. Modern stage theories satisfy a deep longing for a hidden unity that weaves experience into a seamless fabric. We do not like to see anything wasted or thrown away; perhaps that is why the principle of conservation of energy is so aesthetic. The possibility that the intensity, variety, and excitement of the first years of life, together with the extreme parental effort those years require, could be discarded like wrapping paper that is no longer needed is a little too threatening to our Puritan spirit. But given the available evidence, we should at least remain open to that idea.

THE POWER OF CONTEXT

The major disquiet I feel after a study of this creative set of contributions is the omission of references to the power of situational context in infant behavior. The authors treat intelligence, smiling, attention, or fear as if they were attributes of the child rather than the product of interactions between the child and the task context. I noted in a recent paper (Kagan, 1976) that Western psychologists prefer to posit abstract attributes that are minimally constrained by context. One speaks of hostile or depressed people and rarely feels it necessary to specify target and occasion. Mischel's (1968) cogent criticism of this affinity for traits reflects a growing corpus of empirical data which implies that we must specify the target and occasion of motivational and attitudinal dimensions. A similar criticism applies to cognitive competences. Generalizations about memory, reasoning, planfulness, or perceptual analysis rarely specify the problem context in detail or restrict developmental principles to classes of problem situations. There is minimal generality to the concrete operational groupings across different tasks during the transitional period from 5 to 7 years of age. Similarly, quality of recognition memory is dependent on the information to be remembered, as planfulness is dependent on the nature of the task. But we have not applied this new appreciation to the work on infants.

The unpublished results of an analysis of a large body of longitudinal data gathered on over 75 Chinese and Caucasian children who have been observed eight times from 3.5 through 29 months makes this point in bold relief. Several different auditory and visual episodes were administered to the children at each age, and the child's attention, vocalization, fretting, smiling, and motor activity were coded. For example, on one episode the child interacted with an adult female. On another, the child heard taped speech; on another the child was shown a visual event in which a 2-inch block was taken from a box and moved in front of the infant for a series of trials; on another the child saw a small wooden car roll down a wooden ramp and strike a Styrofoam object at the bottom of the ramp. The behavioral variables did not display impressive generality across all of the episodes. A child who was highly attentive or irritable on one episode was not necessarily attentive or fretful on another. There was also a remarkable lack of stability in reactivity across age. Although lower-class children were less attentive than middle-class children to some of the episodes at 3.5 months, there were no class differences in level of attention to the same episodes from 5 through 29 months. Although the Caucasian children smiled more in response to some of the episodes (especially the female examiner and the block episode), they did not smile more than the Chinese in response to the episode in which the car rolled down the ramp. Moreover, behavioral differences between social classes or ethnic groups on a particular test at a particular age often did not occur at another age. Freedman's suggestion that Chinese newborns are less labile than Caucasians on the Cambridge Infant Scale is an interesting and important result. But it does not necessarily mean that lability is a generalized attribute of Caucasian children that will appear in all contexts and at all ages. We must begin to replace statements about abstracted traits with statements about dispositions in classes of contexts.

This volume is one of a series of recent announcements declaring the reunion of psychology with its proper partner. The phenomena we have seen through one lens—crying to separation, symbolic play, or learning to read—suddenly take on an enriching dimension. More important, the empirical probes of these phenomena and the explanations we will accept as satisfying have been profoundly changed. The authors of these contributions have enriched our understanding of development and have hastened the day when the coherences between biological and psychological processes will be less disguised.

REFERENCES

Bornstein, M. H. Qualities of color vision in infancy. *Journal of Experimental Child Psychology,* 1975, **19,** 401–419.

Broman, S. H., Nichols, P. L., & Kennedy, W. A. *Preschool IQ: Prenatal and early developmental correlates.* Hillsdale, New Jersey: Lawrence Erlbaum Assoc., 1975.

Kagan, J. Emergent themes in human development. *American Scientist,* 1976, **64,** 186–196.

Kleinman, A. The cultural construction of clinical reality comparisons of practitioner-patient interaction in Taiwan. Unpublished manuscript, 1975.

Mayr, E. Behavior programs and evolutionary strategies. *American Scientist,* 1974, **62,** 650–659.

Mischel, W. *Personality and assessment.* New York: Wiley, 1968.

Rosenblum, L. A., & Alpert, S. Fear of strangers and specificity of attachment in monkeys. In M. Lewis & L. A. Rosenblum (Eds.), *The origins of fear.* New York: Wiley, 1974. Pp. 165–194.

Schaffer, H. R. Cognitive components of the infant's response to strangeness. In M. Lewis & L. A. Rosenblum (Eds.), *The origins of fear.* New York: Wiley, 1974. Pp. 11–24.

Waddington, C. H. *The evolution of an evolutionist.* Ithaca, New York: Cornell University Press, 1975.

Author Index

Numbers in *italics* refer to pages on which the complete references are listed.

Topical Index